'A riveting story of a true crime, with the pace and dramatic tension of a thriller and a first-rate forensic analysis of the psyche of someone determined to kill those who hold different views from his own.

'*Murder on His Mind* is a perceptive, first-hand account of what it is like to experience trauma, how variously people respond to it and how differently individuals need to work to deal with its impress on their minds, relationships and lives.

'*Murder on His Mind* creates an empathic bridge to understand in an almost visceral way, what the experience of trauma is like and how it transforms perceived reality and sense of self.

'Allanson's book demonstrates how the greatest human strengths of courage, compassion, kindness and commitment to continuing in a workplace suddenly marked by deadly risk, can co-exist with the expression of human frailties and overpowering vulnerabilities more usually associated with violent victimisation.'

Professor Jill Astbury, Australian & New Zealand *Journal of Public Health*

'Allanson depicts with stark reality the perspectives of all involved, the killer, the right to lifers, and the people who need the clinic's services to help them deal with the trauma and tribulations taking place in their own lives. Nobody could read this book and be unaffected.

'[Allanson's] understanding of the ways in which people respond and need to be responded to when under acute stress would provide a very handy manual to anyone who might have to deal with car crashes or any other sudden event leading to unexpected death. Clearly there is an important difference between the accidental and the deliberate killing involved here.

'Much benefit will be obtained from this book by those who are affected by trauma of many different sorts, well away from the setting of the abortion issue.'

Dr Robert N Moles ACII (UK) LLB (Hons) (Belf) PhD (Edin)
Adjunct Associate Professor, Flinders University

MURDER ON HIS MIND

The Story of Australia's Abortion Clinic Murder

Dr Susie Allanson

Foreword by Natasha Stott Despoja AO

WP

Acknowledgement of Country

We acknowledge the traditional custodians of the land on which this book was written. Our country is a land where awful wrongs were done, and continue to be done, to Aboriginal people. We pay our respects to the elders of this country, past, present and emerging.

WP

First published 2006 by Wilkinson Publishing Pty Ltd
This edition first published 2021.
ACN 006 042 173
Wilkinson Publishing
PO Box 24135, Melbourne, VIC 3001, Australia
Ph: +61 3 9654 5446
enquiries@wilkinsonpublishing.com.au
www.wilkinsonpublishing.com.au

First published 2006
This edition published 2021

Cover and book design by Tango Media.
Printed and bound in Australia by Griffin, a Part of Ovato.

ISBN: 9781925927658
A catalogue record for this book is available from the National Library of Australia.

For those who cherish our freedom to choose

&

For our heroes

Author's Note

This re-release by Wilkinson Publishing of *Murder on His Mind* coincides with the 20th anniversary of the tragic events that inspired the original publication, and also coincides with the release of *Empowering Women: From Murder and Misogyny to High Court Victory.* Written with lawyer Lizzie O'Shea, *Empowering Women* is a celebratory sequel to *Murder on His Mind* and tells how security guard Steve Rogers' murder by an anti-abortion fanatic became the catalyst for a successful campaign to protect patients and staff from religious extremists, and for a landmark High Court decision enshrining Australian women's right to reproductive autonomy and respect. Astute observers may note a cover design overlap between *Murder on His Mind* and *Empowering Women* that mirrors the transformation from the chaos of tragedy in the first book to the clear and powerful legal victory in the sequel.

Murder on His Mind is about an actual event, written in narrative form. I have tried to be true to the facts of this case and the people involved, but inevitably I perhaps will have over emphasised some aspects and some people, while unfairly minimising or ignoring others. My apologies to those who feel my account is unfair to them or their experience. I am aware that I could never do justice to the richness and complexity of experience this tragedy brought to each individual. The factual details and personal experiences recounted here are based on information available to me from a variety of reliable sources. My description of the gunman's intrapsychic world is conjecture only drawing from my imaginings and knowledge as a clinician. At times descriptive details and names have been changed purposely to ensure a person's anonymity.

Some symptomatology following exposure to an extreme stress is ubiquitous and often does not require any diagnosis.

There is some evidence that social support, family history, childhood experiences, personality variables, and pre-existing mental disorders may influence the development of both Acute Stress Disorder and Posttraumatic Stress Disorder.

These disorders can develop in individuals without any predisposing conditions, particularly if the stressor is especially extreme.

From the *Diagnostic and Statistical Manual Of Mental Disorders.* (Fourth edition. DSM-IV. American Psychiatric Association. 1994.)

Foreword

In 2006 when this foreword was written for the first edition of Murder on His Mind, *Natasha was the federal Senator for South Australia and Democrats' Spokesperson for the Status of Women. Today, Natasha Stott Despoja AO is a member of the UN Committee for the Elimination of Discrimination Against Women, and 'bubble zones' are known as abortion safe access zones and have rolled out across Australia to protect women and abortion-providing staff from religious extremists.*

This book is about an act of terrorism against women that ended with the death of a man. It is typical of the way terrorism tends to hurt people who have nothing to do with their cause. But the message of this act of terrorism was to women, and it came through loud and clear: there are those who will never permit women to control their own lives and those people will go to any lengths to convey their message. Dr Susie Allanson asks: 'How can such a situation (the killing of a security guard) occur in this day and age in Australia?' But she knows the answers better than most. Through her experience as a clinical psychologist working at the East Melbourne Fertility Control Clinic for 15 years, she knows that women's reproductive rights are still questioned.

Speaking of the killers Susie says in the same paragraph: 'Their intolerance is tolerated… the tacit approval and incitement to violence (is) in the extremity of anti-choice protesters' rhetoric and behaviour.' Our society has permitted this act of aggression towards women. That is not to say that ordinary Australians condone the killing of a security guard. But it is time to end the tolerance that allows extreme acts against women in the home, or elsewhere, by putting them in some special category. Extreme anti-abortion rhetoric has somehow been tolerated as something less than a threat, though that is exactly what it is. Susie describes the daily running of the gauntlet that staff and patients have to endure even to get into the clinic. For doctors and staff, women and their families, it can be a trauma to be endured.

When I have visited the clinic I have also been subject to the harassment and threats, of being accused of 'killing babies' and 'not caring about life'. To walk through the doors of the clinic eight months after giving birth to my son to be told I 'didn't care about the lives of children' enraged me too. Yet, I was not a woman in an emotional, sometimes traumatised, state needing advice and support, nor a woman who had made her clear choice and still had no right to be badgered and demeaned in this way. That is why I will continue to work with the clinic—and many others—to ensure that Bubble Zone legislation is enacted. We might ask why, in this day and age, we have to work for protective zones for women just so they can go about their daily business or carry out their health choices?

Susie Allanson tells the devastating story of the murder of Steve Rogers with reference to the extraordinary way the team at the clinic coped with this act of violence and in the context of the lives of women who attend the clinic. This is so important. Telling the stories of women who need an abortion is something the movement for choice needs to do. It is something we have not done for the sake of putting cool and logical arguments to counter the rampant rhetoric of our opponents. We know that the best true stories from life will help win the day for the pro-choice movement better than anything. It is time women insisted on their stories being told and that everyone from government to angry 'pro-lifers' listen to them. How did they get away with calling themselves 'pro life' when the life of a woman sometimes means nothing to them compared with the potential life of a fertilised egg? When some of them are associated with violence, like that which took away Steve Rogers's life, in many parts of the world?

We should corner them with our truth and experience and demand life and quality of life for women: and that begins with respecting and protecting our reproductive rights and our health choices.

Natasha Stott Despoja AO

Time present and time past
Are both perhaps present in time future,
And time future contained in time past.
If all time is eternally present
All time is unredeemable.
What might have been is an abstraction
Remaining a perpetual possibility
Only in a world of speculation.
What might have been and what has been
Point to one end, which is always present.
Footfalls echo in the memory

T. S. ELIOT
FOUR QUARTETS

Prologue

Somewhere in the Killanbutta State Forest,
New South Wales, Australia
DECEMBER 1999

He tightens his grip on the axe. Calloused hands on warm wood. Smacks it into the tree trunk. Sharp metal on living wood. Three more times, and the giant gum begins its fall, its death throes loud and eerie in the bush stillness.

In conquering the wilderness, he is empowered. His determination and skill are showcased. He knows his stamina and physique are exceptional. The wild does that to you. He knows he needs no one and wants no one. He can cover miles and miles on foot or bike. He is strong, fit and untouchable. He shuns and derides modern society, with its luxuries, pollution, poisons and immorality. He loathes the mundane evils of humankind. And he doesn't need Them.

For ten years this forest has been his haven and his hell. His self-enforced isolation of hard labour has seen him clear an area the size of half a football field, dig a dam, plant fruit trees, fence off sections of land, build his humpy. In the winter, he willingly shares the fierce cold of the night with the over-sized nocturnal rats come scavenging for food or seeking the heat of his fire. In the summer, the sweat pours from him under the relentless, stinging sun.

He no longer knows how it came about. He never really has known. It is inconsequential now. An accumulation of actions.

The unspoken left unsaid. The spoken too hurtful. Words between people are ineffective, difficult, potent. His discomfort in the world of people. His difference, wariness and self-consciousness. Rejected now rejecting. His preference for his own company. There was, and is, nothing out there for him.

So he left. Just like that. He left them all behind. Left the glare of societal niceties he did not understand, a world out of step with him. His social interactions were like ghastly syncopated miscues, jarring, disconnected. He always found himself outside of it all. Outside of community, of love. Not that it really bothered him. They had nothing he wanted and nothing he needed. He saw others committed to romance, family, a career, studies, travel. None of these held any interest—or inspired any passion in him now. He had no need for these. He didn't really get it. He didn't, couldn't, feel it.

So why not finally do the logical thing? Find solace in his own company and his own place within the wild. Something which is his alone, that They cannot trample on, pry into, or take away. He doesn't give a stuff what They think. Doesn't really cross his mind. It is that simple.

And it works. Quiet. Secluded. Alone. Working hard just to survive. Stoic self-deprivation breeding its own contentment. There is a purity in it. No longer constantly facing a mismatch with the world around him. No longer needing to play the game. He could just be him. Be himself. For a time.

But more often lately, his seclusion breeds discontent too. His thoughts keep returning to Them. Those he turned in his back on for a decade. They sneak up on him when he least expects them. He might be tree-felling as he is now, or scavenging for fire fuel, or pedalling hard on one of his irregular sojourns to get the supplies he still requires from sources outside his bush world. One minute he is consumed with just getting it done, oblivious to the sweat on his brow, the ache of his muscles, or the growling of his belly. The next minute, he catches himself thinking of Them—the lusting whores of women and the money-greedy men who, with their poisons and immoral ways, seal the fate of the helpless children.

It seems that he cannot get away from Them. Even out here. Even where he is sequestered and surrounded with a totally different world based on nature and basics and truth. Even here. With not a soul in sight. For miles. Nothing but wild bushland.. Even here They intrude into his thoughts. The more he tries to escape the world of others, and the more he dominates this harsh environment, the more the other world's cruelties, its evils, prey on his mind.

So he puts his intellect to work. He involves himself in long philosophical soliloquies in his mind and develops his ideas. He thinks and writes and thinks and reads. They are highly emotional issues, but the anger deep within him barely surfaces. He barely knows it is there. He does not care where it all came from. Just that it is there. Driving him and pointing the way to a powerful meaning. It becomes an obsession, and he is driven to understand. Hand in hand with his back-breaking manual labour, he embarks on a gruelling mental journey: the meaning of Life, His life, Their lives.

His mental journey brings him in touch with a place he thought he had escaped. A place unknown and disowned. A dark well of anger and arrogance buried deep within his soul. Lying dormant. Fermenting. Waiting. Until the time when his thoughts penetrate into that dark place and tap into an obsessive and violent vengeance.

His disdain for his fellow human beings flourishes. An insidious sense of his own superiority swells into an outraged omnipotence. He recognises how they have betrayed him, and betrayed so many others. Betrayed the most vulnerable. The children.

And then, slowly, a smug realisation takes its place. He mocks the world of people in a way he has not done before. A thrilling sense of revenge is disguised in the garb of philosophical arguments and moral imperatives and godliness. He cannot see it for what it is. He cannot see the contradictions, or his hatred. He cannot see his hurt. He will banish the untouchable feelings inside himself, and inflict them on others. He will be selfless. It will be for their own good.

The stupid, evil bastards. He'll stop 'em.

1

There was the Door to which I found no Key:
There was the Veil through which I
Could not see:
Some little talk awhile of Me and Thee
There was—and then no more of Thee And Me.
RUBAIYAT OF OMAR KHAYYAM

It started for me on Monday 16 July 2001 at 10.40am. For others it started twenty minutes before, ended minutes later, and continued for months, maybe years, maybe forever. For yet others it had not even begun, but it would. And for one it began many years ago, and it is incomplete. It came to be known as 'the abortion clinic murder'. Steve Rogers had his life taken away that day. But in his death Steve prevented it becoming known as 'the abortion clinic massacre'.

It is the first Monday following the mid-year school holidays and I am still in my track pants. When I answer the phone, it is definitely not what I expect to hear. Usually Janice's voice on the end of the phone is upbeat and vibrant. Both in her physical appearance and bubbly personality, Janice shares an uncanny resemblance to Elvis' frequent movie love interest, Anne Margaret. Auburn tresses frame pretty facial features now mellowing into a mature elegance and complimented by chic spectacles. Although physically quite petite, her effervescent personality and job description endow her with a larger stature.

Janice is the manager of the Fertility Control Clinic. She shoulders a rather awesome responsibility in ensuring the smooth running of Australia's first and largest free-standing abortion providing clinic. The clinic was originally set up almost thirty years ago by the late abortion rights campaigner, Dr Bertram Wainer.

In addition to pregnancy termination, women access medical treatment for a wide range of fertility-related health services including the entire range of contraceptive advice and treatment, routine pap smear, sexually transmitted illness screening and treatment, colposcopy, vasectomy for partners, women-centered counselling, an on-site pathology lab, telephone information service, and a 24-hour telephone service. Our staff of thirty includes a gynaecologist, GPs specialising in family planning, anaesthetists, nurses, scientists, counsellors, a Vietnamese/Mandarin interpreter, administrative and reception staff, and me—a clinical psychologist. It makes sense that, worldwide, accessible, affordable abortion providing services usually reduce the abortion rate and improve women's reproductive health.

There is considerable multi-skilling of staff, so that counsellors at times also undertake administrative and reception duties, some nurses are also counsellors, and counsellors often have a nursing background. This means that throughout our clients' initial contact and continuing consultations with us, their needs are met by understanding, experienced staff well-versed in the anxiety and distress often associated with reproductive decisions and medical procedures, especially the rather overwhelming event of finding yourself pregnant when you least expected to be. An unfair societal stigma and fearful mythology still attaches to accessing family planning and abortion services. But our clinic is kept busy with women from metropolitan and regional Victoria, Tasmania and New Zealand, and women whose residence is overseas but who are currently holidaying, studying or working in Australia. It seems that no-one is immune from becoming pregnant when they least expect to. Our service is used by mothers and students, lawyers and shop assistants, doctors and nurses, politicians and school teachers, working girls and police officers. We see the whole range of women of reproductive age.

Our clinic shares much in common with other day procedure and women's health clinics. But a continuing societal climate of secrecy and taboo around abortion and contraception, and the daily clinic vigil by a few picketing pro-life, that is, anti-choice protesters, means that our clinic is also quite different from other day procedure centres. Picketers are present at the front of the building in East Melbourne between 7:30am and 10:00am. Every morning the Clinic is open—six days a week.

We pride ourselves on being genuinely women-centered and genuinely pro-choice in our approach. We will do what we can to ensure that a woman has the opportunity to think through her decision, whether that ultimately is to terminate or continue a pregnancy, and to feel as comfortable as possible throughout her personal journey.

Our staff needs to be particularly well-suited and supported in this unique working environment. And Janice puts staff welfare high on the agenda. She is equally concerned for staff with considerable longevity here, as to those few who start here but decide that for various reasons the job is not for them. The latter have been relatively few. If a staff member leaves because of one or more of the myriad personal moral or other issues around abortion, Janice will offer them a session with me so they can talk through their concerns before leaving.

'They need to sort this out before they move on, don't you think?'

Janice has a knack of knowing when a staff member may be experiencing problems to do with work or to do with their personal life. She knows when and how to ask questions, when and how to listen, and when to tune me in to someone needing a bit of a chat. She usually knows when to stay quiet and when to say her piece. We, her family of staff, are privy and sympathetic to her occasional sighs and grumblings of frustration. Such feelings are after all inevitable for all of us working in this environment. And she knows how to take the mickey out of anyone who might be getting too caught up in their own self-importance. In Janice's teasing, 'Well hello, Ms Allanson,' her 'Mzzzzzzz' takes an emphatic precedence over the rest of her greeting—which seems to have increased since I got my doctorate.

And so Janice holds a position crucial to the lives of countless women and their families. She carries her position with dignity and humour, with sensitivity and business-like assurance. But today as other days, when I hear her voice, I cannot inhibit a flash in my imagination of Janice dressed in a sixties' two-piece bikini and doing the twist with Elvis Presley on a paradise beach.

This time, a lightning bolt immolates the scene.

'Our security guard has been shot. Steve is dead.'

2

Ah Love! Could you and I with Fate conspire
To grasp this sorry Scheme of Things entire,
Would not we shatter it to bits—and then
Re-mould it nearer to the Heart's Desire!
RUBAIYAT OF OMAR KHAYYAM

Fifteen minutes later I am being driven into the clinic. With the outward transformation from track pants to business suit comes an inner restoration. My mind becomes more focused, though a shivering persists. It is nothing but the left over vibrations from my earlier shock, like the drops of water which cling to the swimmer as she slips out of the surf, and walks away from the sea. Then, cool air on wet skin can chill you to the bone. A murder can too.

During the drive I gain strength, focus and some of the professionalism which totally abandoned me earlier. I know I am getting myself into an appropriate frame of mind, shuffling through my clinical knowledge, strategies, approach, until it begins to take on an orderly, logical coherence. Getting in touch with me the clinician, with a job to do. My mind is racing with what I need to put in place in terms of psychological critical incident management. I fumble through my address book, shaking hands dithering with thin pages, disorganised visual scanning failing to find what I seek. There's the name I want. But a recorded message tells me he is in Vancouver at a Posttraumatic Stress Disorder (PTSD) conference—touché. So is another esteemed colleague. I will need to check with police procedure/arrangements in organizing external consultants. The people I bring in have to be right. I know that our staff's wellbeing, and that of patients, might depend on me getting things right in the very early stages.

The drive seems to take for ever. It seems that Time is messing with me. I did not know that Time and Trust were so closely related. Time and Security. Time and Control. Time and Questions. I realise that I know next to nothing about what has happened and when it happened. I know nothing of what to expect when I do get in there. How will staff be? Patients? When and how did it all happen?

I don't know that Janice was in touch with me within half an hour of the shooting. Nor that I will get into the clinic less than one hour after the shooting. I am not to know that in the coming days the quickness of response and strength of character of our staff, our heroes and our families will continue to amaze me and continue to arouse pride.

I ponder on Steve, a 44-year-old father of seven children. He hadn't been our security guard long, less than two months. A quite handsome, outgoing and rather gentle man, not really fitting the security guard stereotype. His friendly manner invited social discourse rather than warned off closeness. Steve stood over six feet tall and carried no excess weight. The formality of his Chubb Security uniform melted with his grin—a grin reflected as much in his light, shining eyes as in his mouth. A grin hinting of the sweet, charmed larrikin of his youth.

During one of our brief chats he'd commented that the anti-choice protesters hadn't given him any trouble. It was the simple, everyday topic of conversation you might have when you are entering your place of work, and your security guard is escorting you through the front gate while a handful of anti-choice demonstrators try to intimidate you out of entering your workplace. Mentally, I shut out their placards, their faces, their taunts, their prayers and singing. I shut out their vile God-speak which shares no resemblance to my ideas of love and compassion. I have no difficulty appreciating that some people do not believe abortion is right, and that some women can never have an abortion, no matter how difficult their circumstances. But most people do not force these opinions onto others by bullying and intimidation. Such actions display disrespect for human life.

On those occasions when I could not avoid this fanatical group, I'd focus on Steve's reassuring presence. Hating having to admit to myself that I loath having to walk past the protesters. Hating the feeling of discomfort. Like the discomfort on rare occasions when one of society's saddest and most vulnerable accosts me for money and invades my personal space with actions and words distorted by drugs, senility, desperation or madness.

So I'd focus on Steve. A grin. A wisecrack. Something mundane and normal. I'd cheekily wonder aloud whether the protesters are still thinking they could convert him.

'No chance of that.' And his grin and chirpy chat blots out their meanness and my discomfort. 'No chance of that.' Steve is immune to conversion, he says. 'I'm an atheist,' he says.

And I ponder that the atheists aren't the only ones. Genuine God-fearing people are insulted by the protesters, too. So is almost everyone—humanitarian, feminist, Buddhist, Jew, Catholic, agnostic, and the whole multicultural, multiracial, multilingual landscape embraced by the term, 'Aussie'. No matter what a person's views on abortion, almost everyone disagrees with the picketers' tactics. Their tactics are unconscionable. 'Murderer,' yells one to a slightly unnerved, mature woman and her now shocked and protective husband. 'Your mother is going to murder you baby brother or sister,' says another to a four-year-old child holding the hand of his mother. 'Do not murder your baby,' whispers another sidling alongside a young woman approaching the clinic and thrusting a pamphlet towards her. The pamphlet is adorned with a photo of a mangled fetus, and provides the reader with blatantly false and frightening information: abortion will give you breast cancer, infertility, mental illness... A variety of A-frame posters sit on the pavement at the picketers' feet—offensive, fanatical intrusions into the everyday lives of people in East Melbourne. One poster, in vivid colour, says it depicts an eight-week embryo and a dismembered fetus. Another poster-sized blackboard screams with white paint, 'the new holocaust at this abortion chamber'. Around the neck of a picketer dangles a relief sculpture portraying stages of fetal development. A wooden cross stands on the pavement facing the clinic gate branded with the words, 'massacre of the innocents here now'. The picketers brandish a cross like a weapon. Sometimes there is violence between the protesters and the public, and the police attend.

Even amongst the protesters, I wonder if some are not as comfortable with the degree of confrontation and lack of kindness shown towards their fellow human beings by some of their peers. Certainly some of the protesters are quieter souls, while others are quite brazen and harsh. But apparently the protesters see no contradiction. They don't see hypocrisy in their actions.

Facing this fraught atmosphere each day, the clinic security guard has to be a certain, special personality. Sheila, a former clinic security guard, was such a person. Sheila could muster a 'don't mess with me' attitude that you wouldn't dare mess with. She was larger than life. Sheila's physical presence was formidable. Pretty features surrounded by a cluster of brunette curls, but with a strong build. And Sheila knew how to use it. A cheeky extrovert, sensational at her job, protective and reassuring to staff and clients alike. Over the lengthy time she served us, she endeared herself to the entire neighbourhood.

During one of Sheila's routine shifts, an anti-choice protester threatened to kill her or have her killed. He also pointed at our senior counsellor, June, who was clearly visible standing inside the clinic garden, and declared her a target too. While June brushed the threat away like a piece of lint from her clothing, Sheila was uncharacteristically distressed. Sheila copped plenty of abuse from the protesters and dealt with it. Although frequently disquieting and distressing to our clientele and to us, the protesters' behaviour rarely suggested that they would actually physically hurt anyone. This protester was different. He was not a regular, and Sheila could see 'evil in his eyes'. Sheila reported this threat to kill to the police. I have no doubt that Sheila was correct in her assessment. I had never before seen Sheila so distressed. To me she always seemed unassailable. Sadly, Sheila left her employ with us.

After Sheila we'd had another female security guard for a while. But she inevitably got caught up in yelling matches with the protesters. Although understandable given the nastiness of some of their comments, such behaviour was not exactly reassuring, helpful or professional. Sheila had already demonstrated that you could carry out these unusual duties with dignity and muscle, while Steve revealed another dignified style as well.

Our first security guard had been a bloke called Dragon with visible tattoos. On entering the Clinic, women would ask if there had been a bomb scare or something equally as frightening. Once we changed to a female security guard, such concerns dissipated. I guess I hadn't been sure how Steve would go, being our first male security guard for a while. I needn't have worried.

Now, less than two months after he took on the job, Steve is gone. A gentle, outgoing man whose job it was to make others feel secure and protected, has been killed.

I feel the sharp tip of that jagged, soul-destroying emotion, anger. The emotion which churns up the insides of so many, with nothing to show for it all, but insides ripped to shreds. The emotion which for years has erroneously been encouraged as cathartic, good for you, get it all out, let it all hang out. Its seduction lies in its energising power. It provides relief and escape from the paralysing black depressions and the unbearable, exhausting anxieties. Anger is the most wonderful and the most destructive life force. It is addictive, exhilarating, and blind to the desolation it leaves in its wake. It is blind to the magnitude and importance of the clean up. The challenge is to harness its power before it destroys you or others.

It digs at my gut with its sharp edges. How can such a situation occur in this day and age in Australia? How outrageous is it that a women's health clinic has to have a security guard anyway? What do these people, who present themselves as peaceful ambassadors of love, protectors of humanity and then spit out biblical words as if they are invective to intimidate and incite hatred, what do they think they are really doing? They don't see this as hypocrisy. Their intolerance is tolerated. Their right to protest apparently protected above all else. The tacit approval and incitement of violence inherent in the extremity of anti-choice protesters' rhetoric and behaviour.

I refocus on what I have to do, what I can do for our staff and our patients, what I need to find out first, who I need to speak with, what I need to put in place. I feel very little, except urgency to be with our staff and get started.

I bring with me a mental image of Steve standing at his post at the clinic gate. Soothing and reassuring our clientele with his smile, his soft word, his physical presence. Steve doing his job. Standing at the gate. Then somehow, awfully shot and killed.

The car radio is on. Is there any more news about Steve's death? Already I am aware that in the rush to get a story out there, the media can inadvertently get both small and more important details wrong. I don't yet know that in the ensuing days such mistakes will at times pose additional challenges for staff and patients, while the media's general endorsement of our role in providing safe, affordable abortion will also uplift staff.

I ponder on the best route to take, unsure if roads will be closed. I don't know what to expect or what is going on. I just have to get in there. Finally we wind our way around Brunton Avenue and the magnificent Melbourne Cricket Ground. The towering stadium with its treed lawns encapsulates all that is beautiful, precious and cherished in Melbourne. The people's ground. We don't just tolerate diversity of dress and thinking and customs and action, we embrace it, revel in it, promote it. One hundred thousand people come together here in hushed silence and then rapturous roaring—100,000 people file in, 100,000 file out. The logistics are momentously and gloriously uneventful. The ground bulges at the seams with the passion, the emotion, the desperate, fanatical cries of allegiance. And then just as quickly The G deflates, spills the crowd from its exits, unharmed, enhanced, generous of spirit. It is more than just a mighty symbol of our country, one of the most laid back, free and inclusive societies of the world. It is that certainty in solid, tangible form.

The MCG is just a hop, step and a jump from the Clinic. Across the busy thoroughfare of Wellington Parade, the railway line and you're there.

There is no traffic jam around this crime scene. We are not delayed by traffic diversions or police checkpoints. Although there will be a huge psychological ripple effect that at times will hit people like a tidal wave, today the area of damage is physically circumscribed and contained. The scene appears to extend little more than one hundred metres along Wellington Parade. I alight from the car less than a block away.

The scene in front of the clinic is busy and cluttered with plain and uniformed police, police cars, areas demarcated with neon police tape, and everywhere is the media, with their cameras, microphones and mobile phones, already filing for their next bulletin. The small shops lining this aspect of Wellington Parade and outside the police tape, are now home to a buzzing media contingent. I already have some sense of the media's potential to swarm and sting. And then just as quickly disperse. The lure of another story. But I also will learn of the media's responsible and sympathetic reporting, mirroring the majority of Australians who believe in freedom and choice, responsibility and privacy.

As I walk towards the clinic, I see some pedestrians looking distressed leaning against a wall outside the main cordoned-off area. I wonder how they might be caught up in all this, whether they will be offered assistance, if they were in some way witness to the crime. Are they partners or friends of our patients? Passers-by? I wonder... and I know nothing.

I approach the first police officer I see, introduce myself and tell him that I want to enter the clinic to be with staff. He speaks with another uniformed officer and points at me, then speaks to a plain-clothes officer and points at me again. Eventually I am cleared to go in, my details are written in a book and I am escorted towards the clinic.

There is no one to hear him, but he expounds his theories anyway. Calls on the night and the heavens, the nature around him, to bear witness to his superior intellect, his sensitive soul, his mighty determination to eradicate the world of these vile slaughterhouse murderers and those who support them.

Occasionally he travels far afield and protests the wrongs of the world. But mainly, he writes it all down. Researches and writes. In the glare of the sun. In the flickering dullness of the firelight. His ideas take over and he is anaesthetised to any discomfort. His precious writing might be for himself alone, or it might be to teach others and to distribute for the benefit of mankind. I bring you good news.

He visits Melbourne to sus out how to disseminate his ideas, get a printer. Flips through the Yellow Pages alphabetised telephone directory. A page or two before her reaches 'Printers', he sees it—'Pregnancy Termination Services'. Disgusting. Awful. Putrid bastards. So this is where we've got to in the year 2000. Telstra's prostitution to the filthy pro-abortionists. Just like the advertisers of the cancer killers. These bloody nongs curry favour for the slaughterhouse proprietors. Drum up trade for the murderers. And what's Optus doing about? Not a thing. And what's anyone doing about it? Bloody nothin'.

It comes to him like serendipity on a spoon. The addresses. Same street. Only meters away. A Telstra business here, and not thirty meters away, the slaughterhouse itself. Wellington Parade, Melbourne. Why not? Why not indeed. What a grand plan. Do one, and then do the other. Or if one is done, does the other need to be done? You bet it does.

And I will bring you good news. And he laughs with a delicious sense of self-satisfaction most people only dream about.

3

Go, go, go said the bird: human kind
Cannot bear very much reality
T. S. ELIOT

As we enter the clinic gate, the beauty of the place is of no consequence to me. But on any other day, it is impossible not to notice the unexpected beauty of a women's health clinic housed in two elegant double-story Victorian terraces which stand within an equally elegant and substantial garden frontage.

In itself, this ambience no doubt has quite profound power to soothe stress and provide solace to those venturing here. The boundary between the footpath and the clinic property is a shoulder high, beige painted brick wall. You enter through a wrought iron gate on the left, at 118 Wellington Parade, or on the right, at 116 Wellington Parade, and follow the bluestone and brick path. The bustle of Wellington Parade with its cars and trams, power lines and concrete, slips away. The senses are filled instead with the clinic garden which is an oasis of lush and mature plants and trees, some flowering, some not, some in huge decorative pots, some reaching deep into the earth with ancient root systems. From tiniest impatiens to tall trees, from the newly planted to those whose life cycle has spanned three centuries. This garden's beauty lies in a heart which invites and nurtures a diversity of genus, colour, scent and age.

A garden bench facing away from the street and towards a small pond has provided a peaceful haven to many a waiting partner, parent or friend. I have spent my share of time speaking with distressed clientele at that bench, the distress either relating to their own circumstances or to the anger or anxieties provoked by the protesters' insensitive or abusive behaviour, comments, leaflets or posters. With a strangle hold on the moral high ground, the protesters see only self-righteous goodness in their violation of normal boundaries of privacy and decency. Their heckles follow patients and staff over the boundary wall like embarrassing and sickening wafts of body odour or rotting garbage. It seems to be some sadistic game to them merely objects, not human, prey to be pursued and persecuted. They show them no respect, no humanity, no decency.

I vividly remember standing at the garden bench trying to calm a near hysterical and crying middle-aged woman. A male protester was yelling over the top of the garden wall at us, 'Don't kill your baby. Don't murder the innocent.' As usual, the protester was so far off the mark it would have been comical, if it were not so tragic. This woman was not pregnant. She was here with her adult daughter. And she was hysterically distressed because with the pro-choice and woman-centered counselling we pride ourselves on providing, her daughter had decided *not* to terminate her pregnancy.

With a police officer, I am escorted up the steps towards the 116 entrance. The two terraces are linked internally to comprise an extensive, modern day procedure centre. A well-equipped, modern theatre with its admissions, waiting and recovery areas, is located on the 116 side. At the 116 entrance is a small reception area and switchboard. The 118 side houses a suite of consulting rooms, a pathology laboratory, main waiting room and larger reception area which is our clients' first point of call. A passage joins the 118 waiting room to the 116 theatre complex, admissions and switch which is bathed in natural light from a picture window behind the receptionist. A grand staircase with a glossy wooden banister extends upstairs from switch. A large, arched window is at the landing, its burst of light and old world grandeur contributes to the building's elegant beauty.

Upstairs, the two buildings similarly become one. But the décor, apart from the beautiful staff lounge with its historic touches, is rudimentary. The staff lounge is above switch, while work and storage offices are also in this right-hand building. My office sits on the other side, above reception. An accounts/administrative office and a smaller tea room also occupy the upstairs of 118. On this side too is a fire escape of stairs leading from the smaller staff tea room to the backyard parking lot.

The police officer pushes open the heavy timber and glass door of 116, and holds it ajar for me to pass inside in front of him. As I enter, I see that Kate is on switch. Kate is a green-eyed, blonde-haired, thirty-something beauty with a quick wit and a wonderful mix of dramatic timing and multi-skilled talents. She reminds us all daily how a sense of humour provides essential benefits. Her greeting to me is upbeat or gentle, light or weary, depending on her day. But always with her own pet name for me, 'Oh, hi Susie Al.' Kate waxes and wanes her way through a day. On the one hand assisting with warmth, sensitivity and nurturance the diverse array of people presenting to her at switch, in a counselling session or in post-operative recovery. On the other hand, suddenly unleashing with colleagues a comedic and sometimes acerbic tongue, or a selection from her wide-ranging repertoire of character mimicry. Here Kate's astute capturing of the quintessence of a person or issue leaves us both gasping with delighted horror and in spasms of hilarity at the shocking truths she reveals in this inimitable way. Now, she looks pale and tired. She has had to face a new shocking truth today.

Homicide squad detectives are flitting in and out, through our clinic. Many staff members are still on the 118 consulting room and main reception side, providing witness statements. One or two are at the St Kilda Road police complex. Janice stands nearby, her face ashen, but alert. She greets me and briefly updates me as best she can. It is only then that I realise that Steve was not shot at his post at the gate outside the clinic, but inside the clinic at the 118 reception. It all happened inside. At reception.

Externally, I barely blink. I am in calm, unshockable clinical mode. I just take it in like everything else, like I expected that to be the case. But internally I have been pushed off kilter. It happened at reception. Not outside, but inside. I have absolutely no idea what has happened here. I must calmly tolerate this fragmentation of knowledge and reality, but I also benefit from having at least a little sense of the much greater fragmentation confronting the majority of staff.

From the edge of the waiting room, I can see a lone chair demarcating the crime scene from the rest of the clinic. Steve's body is out of sight. But I know that it is there. And the knowledge is enough. I have never seen a solitary chair so pathetic and so powerful. Footfalls echo in the memory.

I am introduced to Chief Inspector Brian Rix. In what I quickly come to know as typical of the police working this case, he has a sincere and sympathetic manner. Amidst the dramatic events, he is approachable and professional. He is also media savvy and PR polished.

Chief Inspector Rix is quick to comment on the unpredictable, random and unpreventable nature of such incidents. He lists other Australian tragedies where a lone gunman has intruded on everyday settings to inflict horrendous damage—Hoddle Street, Queen Street, Port Arthur, La Trobe University. Fragments of these shocking events collect collage-like in my mind. The media frenzy, the public disbelief, the outrage, the mourning, the loss of so much.

Strangely, crazily, somehow this helps. It is called perspective. It counters the impact from two potentially devastating waves of aftershock following a trauma. The first is self-inflicted. We should have done that. We shouldn't have done that. What if I'd done this or that? Why did I? Why didn't I? The ruminative doubts and guilt and fears can go on interminably. The second is inflicted by others who unwittingly, or maliciously, blame the victim rather than the perpetrator. Others who exploit this same irrational, erroneous premise of human omnipotence, and hold the victim responsible for what has been perpetrated by another. While we can sympathise with the first, the second is brutal, ignorant and inexcusable.

And so I find some odd comfort in the words of Chief Inspector Rix. And I draw on them in days to come.

I am referred on to Detective Senior Sergeant Lucio Rovis, a man of considerable poise and dedication who in the ensuing days is to become a crucial conduit of advice, and whose crew will leave no stone unturned in building the case against the shooter. To ensure I don't tread on any toes, I mention my wish to bring in consultant psychologists. Is there anyone I should speak with about this first?

Scott Garnett at the Victims Advisory Unit turns out to be a delightfully reassuring and bolstering voice on the other end of the telephone. He rattles off a number of different psychologists' names. I pass over several—this one I know too well, this one is not for us. Finally. Yes. I don't know him personally, but I know of him and he has a good rep. I'll sound him out. Hopefully he's not at that PTSD conference too.

I approach Lou. Although there are three clinic directors—two general medical practitioners and one gynaecologist—Lou is looked on by all as the boss. Lou is a complex man. An astute businessman, perceptive and sensitive practitioner, and teasing stirrer. Short with greying curly hair and a cheeky grin, a twinkle in his eye sparkles with his sharp intellect and sense of fun. Professional and calming with patients, he nonetheless runs on a certain degree of nervous energy. Like all of us, at times this energy spills over. The everyday pressures of Lou's position can be demanding. This would be the case in any women's health centre. But our situation ensures additional pressures. The tiny group of extremists targeting the staff and the clientele of this health centre means that sometimes it is as if we have stepped into a weird twilight zone. In Lou's daily workplace, somehow the Aussie ideals of democracy mean that one quite fanatical group can trample on the fundamental rights and freedoms of the majority. Lou and his family have been the target of rare, but deeply disturbing incidents of violence. I am not privy to the details, the repercussions, Lou's personal pain. Although I might be the first port of call for other staff battling with this life challenge or that, I am unnaturally reticent with Lou. It is a reticence born of the sometimes wobbly line demarcating our working relationship, but also from the private and proud nature of this man and my confidence in his competency. He would include me if he felt it necessary. I can only ponder how confronting today's disaster is, and will continue to be, for him.

Ordinarily, Lou is never short for words. Today he is quiet, composed. I find his manner calming and comforting. I run by him my intention to bring in external consultants. It is essential that I have his OK and his support. There is no hesitation. 'Just do what you have to do, Susie A.' He gives me cart blanche to put in place whatever I feel our staff needs. I feel bolstered and complimented.

As a clinical psychologist with more than twenty years of experience, I'm no slouch when it comes to working with trauma affected people. But this is an entire workplace. And, although I was not in here at the time of the shooting, I am part of all this. I am part of the Fertility Control Clinic team. This is my workplace too. These are my work colleagues and friends. Steve is someone I know.

Still, I can do my bit to facilitate the therapeutic process. It is the little things which will make a difference. I get around to as many of the staff as possible to listen to whatever aspects of their story they wish to tell. I already gently begin the process of normalising their reactions, allaying self-doubts, re-establishing some sense of safety and confidence in our capacity to work this through, bring us together.

June, our Senior Counsellor, is baffled. 'I just don't feel anything,' she tells me. 'Just this nausea. I just can't feel anything, you know?'

Standing five feet nothing in her stocking feet, June is the wise mother figure for us all. Well-dressed, her classy shoes and scarves are her fashion trademark, her dedication and insight her professional trademark. Like many of the middle-aged women who work at the clinic, June has the outward appearance of middle-class conservative respectability. There are no ferocious men-hating, bra-burning feminists here. But we are feminists and humanists just the same. Every day June is confronted with issues that society in general shies away from, stigmatises, or denies point blank. Stark realities of life and human imperfection blow away the secrets of what it is to be a woman in today's world.

Like June, most staff members are in the challenging and privileged position of sharing intimately in women's personal lives in a way which is unique. We are united in our efforts to provide women and their families, often facing extremely difficult circumstances, with warm support, validation and practical assistance. We are united in our disapproval of the protesters' harassing tactics whose 'Right to Life' tag in reality reflects little respect for the right to life of the women and their families who seek health services at our clinic. Perhaps it is not odd at all that our caring, predominantly female and family-oriented staff at times let rip with an exceedingly colourful vocabulary, replete with expletives.

June's clients benefit from her wealth of knowledge, experience and her capacity to assist them through pregnancy and family planning decisions with sympathetic sensitivity, and a refreshing down-to-earth approach complemented with a delightful and wacky sense of humour. She is always aware that despite her own comfortable knowledge of the clinic and every aspect of family planning, this is not the case for each woman she sees. Sometimes it is not just experienced as new and different, but as embarrassing, threatening or frightening. An unplanned, or in some way problematic pregnancy, is sometimes just the visible tip of the iceberg. The iceberg that is too cold, too hard and too slippery to support a woman into motherhood. Sadly, the reality is that the impact of a pregnancy can be traumatic, rather than joyful. The stress levels of women facing a problem pregnancy can be very high, and the sabre-rattling of the picketers can impact disastrously on particular clientele.

She sits in the admissions room. Clearly it is not she who is going to have an abortion. She is of an age somewhere between fifty and sixty. As forms are filled in, she suddenly asks, as so many do, 'Are they always there? The people out the front. Are they always there?'

'Yep. Every morning.'

'Well I don't believe in abortion. I'd never have one myself. But, you know, I'm here to give support to my niece. I might not agree with what she's doing, although gee it would probably destroy her if she tried to be a Mum now, but I don't believe you should tell others what to do. And not like that. They had her crying you know. As if all this isn't bad enough. It's none of their business. They don't know anything about her. She's a good person. And they shouldn't treat her like that. I think they should have a good hard look at themselves. I'd never have an abortion. But I'd never do what they're doing either.'

She is bitter. Very bitter, and desperate. Twelve months ago she was forty. Pregnant. No partner. No job. Living from hand to mouth. Family interstate and busy enough with their own problems. But how she would love a child. This could be her last chance. But how could she cope? What sort of life would that be for a child? Would it be fair? Would it be right?

So she came to the clinic. She spoke with a counsellor about her predicament and was encouraged to think some more about whether to continue or terminate her pregnancy.

Her next clinic visit, they stopped her out the front. She stopped to talk. They promised her what she needed. They promised they would help. She turned away from the clinic. She was going to become a mother.

Now she returns to the clinic counsellor with her babe in her arms—delighted but desperate. The counsellor looks up the clinic resource file and directs her to potential assistance: The Royal Women's Hospital Social Work Department, The Council for Single Mothers and their Children, The Salvo's… But she is somehow falling through the cracks in the system. These days service criteria are strictly adhered to—geographic location, age group, psychiatric diagnosis of psychosis only, etc. There are services for young single mothers, but they do not cater for mature single mothers. There are services for homeless single people but not those with children. And there are waiting lists. She is living in dread that she may lose her child to the Department of Human Services.

'What about your protester friends?' asks the counsellor. 'Have they helped?'

The bitterness is real. The betrayal painful.

'They gave me a bunny and a blanket.'

Each woman who attends the clinic is listened to without censure and is provided with whatever we can which will assist her to find the path which is right for her, with as much comfort and dignity as possible. Most are clear, determined and grateful that the option of a safe abortion is available to them.

'We've only been together three months. I'm 24 and still studying. He's unemployed at the moment and planning to go overseas next month. We used a condom, but it must have broken or something—I don't know. I am totally unready to be a Mum. I have no savings at all, in fact I owe money. My parents are in the country, and Dad's not well. I haven't been able to sleep or eat since I found out. I am just so upset about it. I've always thought that abortion is your choice and that if I found myself in this situation—which I am—then I'm totally cool with that. I didn't think I'd have kids 'til I was about thirty. I know I'm absolutely doing the right thing to do.'

'I've got three children under five. We're struggling as it is. I just couldn't cope with another baby—emotionally I'd go nuts and I don't know how my husband and I could possibly cope. I've got to be there for my kids and I know I just wouldn't be able to do it. I thought that because I was breast feeding I couldn't get pregnant—and I didn't want to take anything that might upset my milk—upset the baby. And now I'm just holding on 'til I can have it done. The nausea is driving me insane. Oh, no—I think I'm going to throw up again… Sorry. Mum's got the kids today so my husband and I could come in together and she totally agrees with me.'

'I was on the pill and I don't know what happened—well, yes, I did go to the doctor a while ago and, yes, she put me on antibiotics… Oh, I had no idea that could make the pill ineffective. Oh, I wish I had known. Why aren't we told these things? Huntington's runs in my family and I have decided that I'm not going to have children. I've thought long and hard about this and I am absolutely sure of my decision. This is a total accident and there is no way I can cope with this. I have to have an abortion—I'll be fine.'

'Well, I kind of got drunk and I was a bit stupid. And I just totally freaked when I realised what I'd done. And I got the morning after pill—but it didn't work. I am so freaked. There is no way I can have a baby. It's my stuff up. My body. Thank God you're here.'

'I'm 43 for goodness' sake. Mum's in hospital and Dad's not coping too well on his own. The kids seem to need me more than ever. I have a back problem… and the chances of abnormalities… and I just can't go back to all that. I just want to get it over and done with so I can get on with things. Oh yes, I'll feel relieved afterwards.'

'My last pregnancy was just a disaster. The labour went on for forty hours and then they finally did a C-section, and then I just didn't cope at all—finally was diagnosed with post-natal depression and we had to go to the sleep clinic, which was a godsend, but I absolutely cannot do that again. My marriage is too important to me, my sanity is too important to me and my two kids are just everything to me. I'm still taking anti-depressants and I see the psychiatrist every couple of months. My husband was already booked in for a vasectomy—how unlucky can you be.'

'What's with the idiots out the front? Like it's any of their beeswax. Can't they find anything useful to do. I know my situation. I've got to live my life. There's no way I'm raising a child as a single mother—it's totally irresponsible. My sister is in that situation and she is doing it so tough and the kids are suffering. I'm not having kids until I'm in a good relationship and well and truly ready. I just can't stand being pregnant. I've been praying that I'll miscarry.'

Some of our clientele are acutely embarrassed and fearful about being here. They come laden with anguish and erroneous beliefs.

Only silly teenagers and prostitutes have abortions; If I have a termination, I'll never be able to get pregnant again; I'll get breast cancer; Women who fall pregnant when they didn't mean to are stupid and don't deserve to be happy; Women who have an abortion never get over it…

The stigma towards abortion is institutionalised in our laws. Like other Australian states and territories, in July 2001, abortion is the only surgical procedure not covered by the Health Act. Instead abortion remains in Victoria's Crimes Act where the Menhennit ruling in R v Davidson (1969) (and the NSW Levine ruling in R v Wald, 1971) stipulates an abortion as 'lawful' when the doctor honestly believes on reasonable grounds that the act is: (a) necessary to preserve the woman from a serious danger to her life or her physical or mental health (not being merely the normal dangers of pregnancy and childbirth) which the continuance of the pregnancy would entail (the necessity test); (b) in the circumstances, not out of proportion to the danger to be averted (the proportionality test), and (c) where the definition of danger to a woman's life or body includes consideration of economic, social or medical reasons.

Often our clients leave us knowing that they are just one of the many lovely people we meet here every day and knowing that no one is immune to the adverse consequences wrought from the complexity of human fertility, relationships and imperfection. Our clients are from all walks of life and from every social class. Ninety per cent of women we see arrive with no doubts about their decision to terminate their pregnancy. They have already discussed their circumstances fully with other significant friends, family or health professionals, and they are confident about their decision and about how they will feel after the abortion. In my work—I counsel the small per cent whose decision and circumstances are particularly complicated—I remind myself that I do not see this vast majority of clear, confident and self-efficacious women—they have no need for me. Nonetheless, the societal stigma of abortion and family planning can still undermine to varying degrees even the most confident of women.

For many women, the stigma of abortion is irrelevant, but they are still facing a physical examination, a blood test or an operation. They may be here for assessment and treatment which has nothing to do with a pregnancy or abortion. Or, although they are here to have a termination of pregnancy and it is one of the safest, simplest and quickest surgical operations (usually taking less than ten minutes and routinely carried out under a general anaesthetic), it is a surgical procedure nonetheless. Women may erroneously think that they will not have an anaesthetic for the operation because of what they have read or heard, and understandably may be fearful about that. Or women may fear having a general anaesthetic, fear a surgical error, or fear the inevitability of being in a situation where they have to relinquish control and are totally reliant on others. Such fears can be quite normal in the face of an impending operation, whatever the operation. But for a few, it can reach phobic proportions. Our counsellors, led by June, provide a crucial service.

June is more than just our senior counsellor. She is an icon of the clinic. Our resident historian, a qualified and gifted celebrant and a pivotal character of the clinic, June was here with Bertram Wainer at the clinic's beginnings. She has lived through the comings and goings of the clinic, the police pay-offs and corruption of the early days, and she has a long memory and a treasure trove of stories. June is always here, always knowledgeable, invincible, indispensable and unflappable. Her emotional stamina leaves us in awe, but also worried. We worry that she takes on too much, that she gives too much and that she does not ask for the respite she needs.

June's celebrant work showcases her sensitivity and insight to the very special meanings of an individual's life and their death. The words flow freely. She brings that person to life by drawing together the poetic and the mundane with her own special gift. The tears fall from the eyes of those whose loss is keen and unrelenting. But her words sharpen the presence of the lost one. Her words are precious and healing. She closes the gaping chasm between feeling and words.

Now, June is bewildered by an absence of feeling, an absence of words. She finds the retelling of her story perplexing. In time, June will find a place for her story within the history she holds. Another chapter of her life where the worst and best in people is documented. And she continues.

So, our staff members bring a wealth of experience as helping professionals working with people facing their own personal crises. Our staff is used to high emotion and seeing others battle with their demons. They are used to being able to support them through difficult times and are somewhat philosophical about the unexpected and shocking kinks in the journey of life. They have skills in understanding and responding effectively to their own and other's needs. We have a wealth of resources to draw on and share with each other.

Our working environment fosters a team of specialists who are perhaps more family, than work colleagues. Like family, there is greater loyalty and bonding between co-workers with significant sharing of our personal lives. Our staff greets the day-to-day challenges of children and partners, work and recreation, as signs of normality to be sorted through and ultimately valued. The burden and the rewards these challenges sometimes impose are more than likely shared with colleagues. But also like family there is the occasional passionate bickering or simmering discontent, and no doubt there is the potential for the latter to follow us into our response to this trauma.

Today we are united in the shock, sorrow, anger, fear, relief, and the strength that this 'critical incident' has and will continue to unleash. We need to harness our strength as a group. We all need to come together as a whole as soon as is practicably possible. More formal debriefing will come just days later, with experts I expect to be the best in their field, up to date with the latest research and providing experienced clinical judgment. They will emphasise balance and strength, and will facilitate, educate and bolster rather than pathologise. They will be aware of the fact that while the majority will find talking about it helpful, a few will be at risk of being retraumatised by talking about it. Despite harnessing the strengths we have as a group, they will be aware that there still might be interpersonal issues which this trauma might exacerbate, and which might undermine the healing group process. Normal recovery and reliance on existing support systems will be enhanced, while questions about the timing and need for more intensive, individual assistance will be addressed.

Homicide squad detectives are still taking statements from staff. Tam, our Vietnamese and Chinese interpreter and receptionist, is in at the St Kilda Road police complex, as are some others. No one seems too sure where Greg is. A laid back, intelligent and casual man, Greg is the youngest of the medical directors. He is slender and slightly gaunt, from his long distance running. His reserved manner and sometimes bright-eyed eagerness and quick-witted jibes make him a popular but low-key member of staff. For a short time, I worry about where Greg is. How he is doing.

Like everyone else, Greg is caught up providing a police statement, and eventually turns up. Like everyone else, he has his own unique story, some lines of which he will tell, some he will not. Some he will share now, some later. He will choose carefully who he tells what, when and why. His own experience to process and reconcile. But, just like my goal for everyone else, I aim to have Greg feel confident that he will sort this through and feel confident that someone is there if he needs them.

The twenty staff in here at the time brings a complex jigsaw puzzle of experiences. Each staff member brings another fractured piece to the complex whole. One thing is clear—it was quick and it was devastating.

4

'Tis all a Chequer-board of Nights and Days
Where Destiny with Men [and Women] for Pieces Plays:
Hither and thither moves, and mates, And slays.
And one by one back in the Closet lays.
RUBAIYAT OF OMAR KHAYYAM

The appointments list is headed, Monday 16 July 2001. It is a Monday morning like any other at the Fertility Control Clinic.

Tam, our interpreter, is at reception today. Tam is Vietnamese Australian. She is almost thirty but looks younger. Clear complexion and silky black hair, her delicate physique and sweet, generous disposition arouses a nurturing, mothering countenance from staff towards her. Her English is dainty, with the delightful lilt of a Vietnamese childhood.

As patients enter 118, the reception desk is on their left. Tam stands behind the reception desk and greets them with a gentle smile and a soft diligent focus, 'Hi, how are you? Do you have an appointment? What is your name? Could I have your Medicare card please?' Between the formal details being written down on the patient card, some casual banter to try and put this woman at ease.

The clinic tones are deliberately muted—beige, greys and soft pinks. Thanks to June, two small vases of pretty flowers sit on the reception desk. Every Monday morning, June picks up a selection of flowers from a favoured florist and arranges then in enough vases for the reception areas and the consulting rooms. Their delicate patterns of scent and colour soften the sharp edges of anxiety which frequently sit on the already overburdened shoulders of our guests.

Many years ago, I was present when a female protester rudely stormed through reception, ranting loudly, and deliberately knocked over the vase, its contents spilling onto the desk and to the floor. Her actions were a mix of the ridiculous and the disgraceful. A violation of June's gentle actions.

At quiet times of the day, June's affinity with plants extends to the clinic garden. June can be found in the garden, hose in hand, tending and caring, enjoying the beauty here. Occasionally in the early morning, as is wont to happen with garden hoses, the spray of water may misfire over the brick wall. Oops, the protesters' exuberance is dampened a little?

Past reception is the main waiting room, where chairs hug the walls and encircle a coffee table awash with magazines. An information display hangs on a wall. 'Pap smears and you' by the Victorian Cytology Service, 'Che cosa fare se il pap test rivela anomalie?' by the Anti-Cancer Council of Victoria, 'Make sure you're right to drive' by the TAC, our own 'Patient Information' brochure. A myriad array of information pamphlets beg to be read. Off this room, one doorway leads to the consulting rooms and pathology lab, and another doorway leads to the theatre complex.

Lining the wall of reception are four tall grey filing cabinets. Unlike the modern décor-enhancing filing cabinet, these are basic and rather ugly. Their external banality gives no hint of the treasure trove contained within. The mundane and morbid, the anguish and passion, the elation and despair, the health and sickness in the minutiae of women's lives. Closely packed patient cards. Each summarising a person's life on a stapled set of white, yellow and blue cards, and a variety of medical stationary. Perhaps the filing cabinets are more sturdy protectors than ugly misfits.

On this morning, like any other morning, Lou finishes a consultation and shows the patient to a seat in the hallway outside his room. He walks with the patient's card down the hall away from reception in the direction of the far consulting room usually used by Kate, and the clinic back door— 'the staff entrance'. To access this from outside, staff and patients must walk down a bluestone lane running along the length and side of the clinic from Wellington Parade. Lou turns off into the short passage leading to the main lab. Three female scientists work here today. Two at separate desks adorned with a variety of scientific paraphernalia. The third about to draw blood from a patient who has lain her coat over the back of the chair. It is a busy and essential little section of the clinic somewhat secreted away here. The walls are a mish-mash of stats sheets, social appointments and photos of pets. The latter belies the serious nature of their work and provides light relief and camaraderie. Anais, the chief scientist, is a striking woman, her Greek background evident in her glossy dark hair with added auburn highlights, and her large, dark eyes. Anais' extraversion and dazzling smile are somewhat at odds with the usual stereotype of a scientist. Her younger colleagues are supervised by her with a mix of good-natured humour and motherly no-nonsense wisdom and encouragement. One is in her late twenties, while the other is even younger. They are both competent in their jobs, a little shy with other staff, but comfortable in their role and interactions with each other and Anais. Anais has built a good team here and is dedicated both to best practice standards and to her staff welfare. All hark from obviously different ethnic backgrounds. All Australian. All work as a co-operative professional team.

Lou starts back up the hall towards reception to pick up another patient card.

June, senior counsellor, is ensconced in her room next door to Lou's. June has already counselled several women this morning. Most women present clear in their decision, and with supportive family or friends, so the counselling session is a chance to exchange pertinent information, ensure informed consent and future contraceptive needs, and provide the opportunity for more detailed discussion if required. But with June now is a woman adamant that terminating the pregnancy is the best option, but extremely distressed. Tissues exit the tissue box in rapid succession, to enter the bin in a tear-soaked state. Her muddled thoughts spill out onto the counselling room floor in a ghastly mess of anguish. June patiently and gently attempts to retrieve from the floor each of the threads of emotional upheaval. She attempts to inspect them separately and ponder, with this woman, how they may weave together into a more meaningful whole. But it is a complex pattern of clashing emotions and events. It is not easy to disentangle let alone to reweave. This pregnancy is intrinsically and powerfully connected to central issues about this woman's very identity and sense of self. She is highly vulnerable. Decisions about a pregnancy can be pragmatic and straightforward or a perplexing riddle demanding the answer to the meaning of life. A pregnancy/abortion decision can be aggravated by its inherent time limit, competing demands of children, job, study or other responsibilities, and in the case of our rural and interstate patients, the additional burden of geographic dislocation. The latter can place even more pressure on financial resources and feelings of isolation and alienation while making this important decision.

'You really have an awful lot to sort through here,' suggests June kindly, but firmly. 'You really don't seem ready to go through theatre. Would you like to think about it a bit more? We could make a time for you to speak to Susie, our psychologist.'

But the woman's circumstances, if she continued her pregnancy, are so daunting that she remains determined to go through theatre today. And June is aware of the importance of respecting a woman's own self-determination and competence, and of the clarity which can ensue when a woman is given the opportunity to proceed to theatre.

'You know you can opt out at any stage. Any time you like you can say that you've changed your mind. Right up until you are under the anaesthetic.'

Seated in the hallway is a mother and her daughter. They wait. Anxious but hopeful. The daughter is just seventeen years old and unexpectedly pregnant. She is clear that she cannot cope financially or emotionally with becoming a mother at this stage of her life; clear that terminating her pregnancy is best for her, her family, her boyfriend and any children she may have in the future.

In some ways, she fits the stereotype of a woman who has an abortion. A stereotype which can arouse embarrassment and shame in those women attending for pregnancy termination who do not fit this distorted norm. How often have I seen women who think that abortion is only for 'silly little teenagers' or prostitutes. How often do I see the sparkle of surprise which accompanies that wondrous 'ah ha' phenomenon, when I spout demographic truths rather than fictions? When the clinic was the secretariat of the Abortion Providers Federation of Australasia, I managed to cajole and organise several private abortion providing clinics around Australia to collect basic demographic data on over 2000 women attending for an abortion. The data was consistent with another published Australian study, and the simple information gleaned was fascinating and instructive. Providing basic data to women helps to demystify and destigmatise abortion and the women attending for an abortion. Of all women who have abortions for psychosocial reasons, over half are in their twenties. Frequently these women may be in an intimate relationship but are not ready to become parents. More than one quarter are women in their thirties or forties, where existing family responsibilities are more likely to play a role. Teenagers account for just one in six, and those younger than sixteen comprise less than one percent of all women attending for an abortion. And we see women from the full range of occupations. Saleswomen, lawyers, at home mothers, doctors, couriers, managers, politicians, nurses, students. 'Working girls' are an oddity rather than the norm.

The 17-year-old is fortunately surrounded in her life by people she can talk to, who love her. She is very early in her pregnancy. She has not felt she must hide from facing the challenge of this crisis, and she is supported by her boyfriend, grandmother, aunt, mother.

But sadly, in her seventeen years she has seen more of the dark side of life than anyone would wish to see in an entire lifetime. Her physical appearance gives no hint of her emotional fragility. She is on an up curve of a vicious weight cycle, which mirrors a roller coaster emotional cycle and tactics of excess and asceticism, from food obsessed gorging to food self-denial. She has not yet succumbed to other forms of physical self-harm. Although, once, she held the flame of a cigarette lighter under her hand and trance-like watched and waited as its pain brought her back in touch with her body, her self, her being. The flame of life, she thought. Momentarily. Then, the flame of Hell. But she has not done that again. And she has never cut herself, cut her arms, breasts, stomach, as some do. She has not got caught in the numbing of feelings, the faked reality of emotional pain transcended through drug intoxication. She would never do that.

She is still in school. Just. She is finding it harder to concentrate and harder to find the meaning of her studying and the point of doing anything. She knows that she has been giving those who love her a hard time—pushing them away with her sullen silences and then her overwhelming demands. She cannot speak the unspeakable. She does not want to think the unthinkable. She rants and raves at the world. At God. Then shuts down. Shuts out. Herself. Those who love her. The rape.

So she sits. Waits. Fears.

Susan, one of our counsellors, is in the consulting room usually used by our gynaecologist. Susan is speaking with a young twenty-something woman who is accompanied by her mother. Anna is thirteen weeks pregnant. Her pregnancy's later gestation already sets her apart from the majority of women who attend with an unplanned or problem pregnancy. Ninety-six per cent of women present prior to twelve weeks gestation, and most of these women present closer to six weeks than twelve. Anna is still agonising over her situation. This continuing ambivalence also sets her apart from most women who reach a clear determination about terminating their pregnancy following the initial jolting shock of finding themselves unexpectedly pregnant, or for a small few, finding themselves confronted with unexpected and seriously changed circumstances in the aftermath of a planned pregnancy. Prior to attending our clinic, most women discuss their situation with their partner, select family members or friends, perhaps a doctor or Family Planning Victoria counsellor. They are relieved to find out that an early abortion is one of the safest and simplest operations (requiring them to be under a general anaesthetic for only 5–10 minutes, or sedation with a local anaesthetic if medical or other circumstances recommend that), and that most women are back at work the next day. They think and talk through the realities of their circumstances and their coping capacity and find strength in their ability to pursue a decisive course of action. They are thankful and relieved that the option of pregnancy termination is available to them, and they respond with relief and improved functioning following the abortion.

Anna has ventured down all these demanding avenues of discussion, information, soul searching and supportive counselling. But she still is not really clear about what to do about her pregnancy. She would love to continue her pregnancy but to do so would impact disastrously on many people, including herself and the child at the end of it all if all went well with her pregnancy. She is not at all clear that she could cope emotionally or financially. She is aware of the important and demanding responsibility of having a child and she, like everyone contemplating parenthood, wants to be the best parent she can be. Her unplanned pregnancy has caught her seriously under resourced. She is not ready to be a mother. She has serious doubts about her capacity to be a good mother, given her lack of stability and readiness.

The expression of Anna's ambivalence and the issues underpinning her ambivalence are totally different from those being discussed in June's room. Anna is still see-sawing in her decision. At times she feels equally drawn to the two opposing states of continuing the pregnancy and terminating the pregnancy. At times, she feels equally repelled by the two opposing states of continuing the pregnancy and terminating the pregnancy. At times, she is drawn more closely to one. Then, soon after, is drawn to the other.

Like many women presenting later in a pregnancy, there is a positive correlation between Anna's longer gestation and her painful indecision. But pregnancy ambivalence is not invariably the reason for later presentation. Women presenting later than the norm may do so for a multitude of reasons. My own mental filing cabinet is strewn with diverse cases. Some so much later than Anna that abortion is no longer an option. Sadly, all it takes is a quick riffle through my mind.

She is forty-five, married with teenage children. Her pregnancy is initially misdiagnosed.

'You're probably going through early menopause,' says her doctor. Not even a thought of a pregnancy test.

But finally her own nagging realisation wins out. And she finds out she is pregnant. Now weeks have passed since her first visit to her doctor. She is panic-stricken. She has completed her family, cares for an elderly parent, has increased career responsibilities, and recognises serious health risks to herself and the potential child if she were to continue the pregnancy. But now, rather than a simple decision and simple surgery, we must refer her elsewhere, where her higher risk age group will provide the reason for her to have a later termination. Sadly, there are more like her.

She is twenty-three. An elite athlete. Talented, dedicated, hard-working and the almost perfect physique. She is the whole package. A coach's dream. A teammate's dream. The calendar guiding her life revolves around world championships, Olympic trials. Like so many other women, for a variety of reasons the most ancient, mystical calendar of all appears to her as indecipherable runes. Her exercise regimen and diet mean that her periods are irregular—she can go for months without having one. She dismisses her bodily symptoms as the flu or stress. Finally she goes to her doctor. Her abdominal muscles are so taut that her pregnancy cannot be detected by a doctor's touch. By the time she visits us she is twenty-two weeks pregnant. And there is nowhere for her to go. Goals she has worked for all her life, goals attainable only within a very restricted window of opportunity dictated by age, skills, physical health and strength, Olympic games and World games calendars. All gone. A condom failure. She is single. Her finances are minimal and geared towards supporting her sporting lifestyle. Motherhood does not on her agenda. Will she be able to survive mentally with the sense that her life is totally out of her control? She feels she has just lost her whole life.

They have been married two months. She has been diligently taking the pill. But she is prescribed antibiotics for an infection and is not told that antibiotics can disrupt the effectiveness of the pill—she should keep taking the pill but also use an alternative method of contraception. She cannot understand how she became pregnant. Their local doctor fills them with ideas that abortion is dangerous. Their desperate conviction that they are not ready for parenthood finally drives them to come into our clinic anyway, and they arrive scared and frantic. They are relieved at the knowledge and treatment they receive. They are relieved that a safe procedure ensures that she is back to an unpregnant state. But they have suffered unreasonable and needless anxiety. She has lost her job in the process. Their relationship almost collapsed.

And there are others like them where belated attendance reflects compelling desperation in the face of their initial terrified acquiescence to the tiny, perhaps well-meaning, but highly dangerous group of professionals and non-professionals who betray their positions of trust, authority and influence. Who subtly sow seeds of doubt about the safety of abortion, or brutally bombard with myths and misinformation about infertility, death, Hell.

No wonder that we also see too many faces, of those old and young, who like the proverbial emu, hide their heads deep in the sands of busyness, depression or denial. Hide from the real world, hide from the truth that they are indeed pregnant. It is too shocking to contemplate and too difficult to overcome. Until finally, if they are to avoid suffocating death, they surface to the real world, swallow in their surrounds. Burning gulps of cold air. Blinks against the brilliant light. Help me. Before it's too late.

Anna has stared into the glaring truth of her pregnancy over many weeks. Despite all her best efforts, Anna finds herself consulting us, still unclear, still unsure. The chances are high that after her initial consultation, Anna will find herself consulting me. She fits the criteria of ambivalence and anguish usually characterising those women who are referred on to me. Although initial uncertainty about what to do is common, continuing ambivalence is a risk factor for post-operative emotional problems. Before a woman proceeds to theatre, it is important that she has reached a point of feeling reasonably comfortable with her decision, confident it is the right decision given her circumstances and is optimistic about how she will be following the abortion. Hopefully she views her decision as affirming what is important in her life now and in the future—her children, relationship, health, study, career, the opportunity to confidently have children in the future and so on.

But for now, Anna sits in a consulting room at the beginning of a journey the end point of which is uncertain.

This morning, these women stand out from the bulk of women who attend the clinic clear in their decision and self-efficacious in their approach to consultations and theatre. That such women comprise only a small minority is no consolation. We struggle to provide them with the emotional relief they seek. We give them a disproportionate amount of our counselling energies and concern. The option of a referral to see me will be discussed. There is no way of predicting when, or how many, more needy clients will attend on any given day.

So, this morning at 10:15am, morning tea is looking pretty good. Steam won't only be coming from the cups of tea and coffee. Staff will be letting off some steam of their own. Awareness of the complexity of human lives. Awareness of all that we do not know and cannot do. Mulling over how to better meet the needs of these women. Knowing that there are just situations where the unfairness of it all makes desperation and heartache unavoidable. Knowing that for these women there are long standing issues which have been avoided, denied, shut away, but which suddenly are demanding immediate resolution or else this major life decision cannot be resolved. A major life decision where there is an unfair time limit. Still, these women must take time to think. This is not a time for rash decisions made out of fear, impulse or for short-term relief. There must be time to think. And so they are urged to do just that. Their cards detour into the 'To Think' box.

The To Think box is our own little Twilight Zone for cards in limbo. Unfortunately, it means that a woman's life is in limbo too. The To Think box embraces the intrigues and woes of the woman who presents with particularly complex circumstances, or who requires additional time to think through her decision. The To Think box cradles her securely until, with the opportunity to talk through her decision, gain pertinent facts, do some homework, take her time, she ultimately decides to continue her pregnancy, terminate her pregnancy, or cannot decide and continues her pregnancy by default. A woman's card might lie in the To Think box for a few hours, days, weeks, or never progress beyond that point. The To Think box is a fascinating space where patient cards sometimes can seem more like playing cards involved in a game of chance and dare, luck and fate. But for the person whose name graces the card, it's no game. It's real.

Ultimately it is up to each woman to assess the odds and make her final decision. A woman whose card makes its way into the To Think box often needs additional assistance. She and her partner may require more than the usual information and discussion about the medical procedure, contraceptive options, views on abortion, her situation, support agencies. She may require substantial information about what we know of the risk factors for suffering post-operative emotional distress and be assisted to relate these to her own unique circumstances. We can facilitate her speaking up about the numerous unspeakable events, fears and feelings, which when spoken and shared can lose some of their terror, self-condemnation and power. She then might be able to consider her options more clearly and honestly. She, sometimes with her partner, can be helped to consider a different perspective of her situation and her resources, different strategies they might utilise. While they may have a picture of their predicament taken from one angle, they can be encouraged to take snapshots from alternative perspectives to study and assess, accept or reject. They can take home literature to read and discuss, consider information about agencies and professionals suiting their particular needs and her treating doctor can be kept informed. But probably our most important function is communicating our respect for her, her partner, and their efforts to sort through a tough situation.

This Monday morning Susan has been providing a crucial part of this counselling process. The clinic day starts early, so by 10:15am Susan has seen a number of patients. Listening, learning, informing, validating. Now, Susan provides pertinent literature to the young woman and her mother and exits the room to allow some time for them to read and talk.

'Poor little thing,' thinks Susan.

Susan is a beautifully groomed woman. Statuesque, fit, effervescent, and modern. She is tanned and trim all year round and wears her youthful clothes with style. Although accurate, the term 'middle-aged' is nonsense when applied to Susan. Her voice matches her appearance. Beautiful diction with a sing-song, vibrant lilt, and laughter which is happily contagious. She exudes warm professionalism, whether in the counselling room or on switch, 'Fertility Control Clinic. Susan speaking.' But bubbling just beneath the surface competency and confidence, is a touch of anxiety and a joie de vivre playfulness, both of which add to Susan's likeable and caring nature. Susan has worked at the clinic almost as long as June has. Where June's longevity reinforces the solid stability and good-natured endurance of the Clinic, Susan's longevity highlights its youthful freshness and vibrant modernity.

Susan leaves her charges alone to read and talk, walks through the main waiting room and into the short hall with the admissions office on one side and the windowed garden and switch on the other.

Tracey is in the admissions room. She is scooting back and forth from here to the small administrative office next to June's consulting room. Efficient and bold, Tracey carries out a multitude of administrative and secretarial tasks. There is something of the surfie chick about Trace, with her long bleached blonde hair. But this woman in her late thirties is a no-nonsense, lets-get-down-to-business person, whose speedy and capable approach means that she does the work of two, and suffers fools lightly. There is a sense that her spit-spot manner emanates from the school of hard knocks, and there is no doubting her generosity. A sense of humour which can be outrageous in its language is softened in her professional dealings with clientele. But outside this gambit, Trace is blessed with being able to call a spade a spade in a most inimitable fashion. Whether she is scathingly describing someone as 'being so far up themselves they need a compass to find their way out,' or gently encouraging someone along with an 'all right, my lovie' or 'cheers, lovie,' Trace is her own person. One senses an endearing vulnerability kept well under wraps.

At switch, Susan finds Janice giving final instructions to someone making a phone booking for a pregnancy-related appointment, 'You'll need your Medicare card, an early morning urine sample and a $25 counselling fee'.

Just across the passage, in the theatre complex, doctors operate in theatre and nurses care for patients in recovery. Women sleep or slowly wake from their anaesthetic induced reveries. Nursing staff take vital signs and eventually, behind curtains drawn around beds, assist patients back into their street clothes and then into the post-operative lounge. Here, their post-operative haze recedes in the face of welcome greetings from a partner, parent or friend, and cups of coffee and biscuits provided by Kate. And when they are ready, in her quiet, professional way, Kate goes over post op instruction handouts with each woman individually.

The routine of the clinic means that at this time of day, some medical staff are upstairs on their morning tea break. In the upstairs lounge, Kathy sips her coffee. She looks relaxed and almost teenage in her baby blue theatre garb, her brunette hair pulled back in a pony-tail, and her intense sparkling eyes peeking out from beneath a thick fringe. By virtue of being our only female doctor, Kathy is an incredibly precious resource. Women who have a history of sexual abuse may be particularly reassured by being examined or operated on by a female doctor. The normal anxieties about handing over control to be physically examined or undergo surgery may reach phobic proportions in women who have suffered abuse. Sometimes this fear initially confounds accurate diagnosis of a woman's decision certainty. Her fear can create the impression of decision ambivalence where in fact she is very clear about terminating her pregnancy. She is just so scared stiff—the actual operation seems insurmountable.

Sadly, our own experience and statistics from Australia and overseas tell us that probably more than 10% of women report a history of sexual abuse and about 40% report having been the victim of physical violence. The statistics are shocking, as are the personal stories of the women who suffer such trauma. Like the 17-year-old sitting in the hallway next door.

Kathy's value is increased one hundred-fold given her outgoing and hardworking nature and the passionate commitment she exudes for her work. These attributes mean that at one stage she was flying regularly to Tasmania each week to provide a much-needed abortion service. In the intervening years since, a standalone abortion providing clinic was both established, and folded, in our smallest Australian state. We have returned to the situation where women with or without their partners or families fly over Bass Strait to Melbourne to attend our clinic before flying back to face the extra bills and work lost. In the coming months, cruel and ignorant political scampering of powerful anti-choice lobbyists will see Kathy again take on the gruelling timetable of weekly visits to the Royal Hobart Hospital.

I routinely marvel at Kathy's unique importance to the women and families we see, and marvel at her dedication as a female doctor in this field of medicine avoided by so many others. Kathy takes a healthy professional pride in her work, with no hint of condescension or conceit. I wonder whether Kathy truly appreciates her special role. To her it is the norm, it is what she does, who she is. So today, like other days here, Kathy takes a theatre break, sips her coffee and contemplates the mundane, rather than the extraordinary.

At 10:15am on this busy Monday morning, Lillian and her partner, Sandro, enter reception. By 10:15am, the anti-choice protesters have left for the day. Lillian and Sandro do not encounter the insensitive and cruel behaviour confronting earlier patients as they enter the clinic gate. Their nervousness is not exacerbated by protesters intruding rudely into their physical and psychological space. Their sense of worth and self-efficacy is not compromised or undermined by complete strangers trying to involve themselves in a private, personal and perhaps difficult experience. At around ten o'clock each day the protesters figure they have 'saved' whoever they can (which is usually no one), anyone attending for theatre would already have arrived, and they leave. So Lillian and Sandro feel no need to avoid the front entrance by accessing the clinic by the staff entrance at the rear. Nor are they greeted by a security guard at the clinic front gate. The departure of the protesters signals the end of the clinic security guard's shift. Steve Rogers has finished his clinic work for the day.

Lillian and Sandro enter the door at 118 and approach Tam at reception. Lillian is fifteen minutes early for her 10:30am appointment, and Tam initially cannot find Lillian's name on the appointment list. Nevertheless, Tam starts to fill in a patient card for Lillian.

It is then that Lillian realises she has left her Medicare card in the car. Sandro responds by leaving to fetch it from their car parked opposite.

As Sandro exits reception, Steve enters reception from the direction of the consulting rooms. Tam knows that it is Steve's routine to come inside at the end of his shift. He goes to the bathroom and says his goodbyes. But Lillian is surprised to see a security guard and doesn't understand why he is here. But it is of no consequence. She has more important things on her mind.

Lillian is seventeen weeks pregnant and committed to continuing her pregnancy. But her situation is complex and she and Sandro need the opportunity to talk some issues through and work out their priorities and some coping strategies. Sadly, media and other societal representations of pregnant women and mothers perpetuate an idealised and unattainable motherhood mythology. All pregnant women glow in radiant health. All pregnant women are blissfully happy. Family and friends of pregnant women rally around to bolster, educate and support unequivocally. All mothers live idyllic lives where they competently and happily love and care for those they adore, while they are adored in return. Aggravation from family, friends, divorce and step-families does not occur. Death, illness and other losses never happen. Financial, study and job pressures do not exist. And so it goes on.

In more recent years, the motherhood myth has come to incorporate the superwoman myth where mothers also manage effortlessly to hold down glamorous careers wearing immaculate, but still sexy, business suits. The fatherhood myth of always in control and consummate financial provider more recently incorporates the hands-on sensitive father. Time is limitless. Energy unbounded.

But what happens when personal experience does not live up to this ideal? What happens when the reality of impending parenthood, even when meticulously planned, eagerly anticipated and with everything in place, confronts prospective parents with anxieties and challenges they had not anticipated. To acknowledge such difficulties is not so easy, to speak of such things is even harder. Confiding in nearest and dearest may not be the best plan - indeed nearest and dearest may be part of the problem. Similarly a woman's doctor may be part of the problem or may not have the time or the requisite counselling training.

But it is imperative that prospective parents can talk to someone. Airing concerns with a nonjudgmental and skilled counsellor can clarify issues and help devise strategies to ease the pressures and instil optimism. After an initial consult today, and given all that is on their plate, it is likely that Lillian and Sandro will find themselves consulting me.

At 10:15am on 16 July 2001, Lillian stands at reception. Nervous about confiding in a complete stranger, but prepared and hopeful.

5

At the still point of the turning world. Neither flesh nor fleshless;
Neither from nor towards; at the still point, there the dance is
T. S. ELIOT

Someone enters the reception door and stands behind Lillian. Tam initially thinks it is Lillian's partner returned with the Medicare card. A glance up from the patient card she is diligently filling out for Lillian. No. It is not Lillian's partner. Another man. Older. Bearded. Scruffy.

Steve, wearing his Chubb security uniform, appears beside Tam. Steve greets the newcomer, 'Can I help you?'

This in itself strikes Tam as unusual. Steve is meant to be leaving for home. His job is not to attend to people at reception. But although there is some sense by Tam that this is strange, she and Lillian concentrate on completing the patient details. They do not hear the man's reply to Steve's apparently innocuous enquiry.

The casual and unhurried quality of the interaction between the security guard and the man behind her, strikes Lillian as somehow odd. She turns to look over her shoulder and sees a man, unkempt and derelict. She does not notice that he is wearing gloves. But she observes that the man has an open hessian bag. The security guard's voice continues calmly. Tam and Lillian continue to engage in the patient card routine. Question. Answer. Pen to card.

'Date of birth?' Gun. Answer. Shoot. 'Date of birth?' Reply. Reply?

The scruffy man has used the words 'gun' and 'shoot'. But his tone is careless, nonchalant. It makes no sense. Such contradictions are to be dismissed. Aren't they? Lillian cannot make sense of what is happening. Just answer the receptionist's question.

But the apparently casual banter, the security guard's calm voice, the other man's words, insist on penetrating Lillian's world. They niggle and nag. Push Lillian slightly off balance. Something is out of kilter. The solid ground beneath her feels unsteady.

Steve's voice, 'Are you serious? Are you for real?'

The answer, 'Yeah, man. I am for real.'

Steve again, 'Are you serious?'

Lillian becomes all flesh and all blood. Bones and nerves and tissue. She has a disturbing knowledge of her internal organs. Her heart rebels. Plummets to her stomach. Blood pumps wildly in misguided madness. Face bleaches white. Eyes redden in terror. Reality whirls into the surreal. Lillian is at the shocking intersection where human helplessness meets evil intent. The space where all time is eternally present and all time is unredeemable. Neither flesh nor fleshness. Shocking violation.

Sandro reappears outside the reception door. Lillian's desperation at the imminent danger is lit up by another shot of adrenalin as she sees Sandro on the threshold. He is on the threshold. Why did you come now? I don't want my loved one hurt. Go, she silently screams. Go. Then, I need you. Don't go. Make it all right. Sandro is her lover and her love. He is strong and big. His presence comforts Lillian, brings some relief to this insanity. Go. Go, my darling.

Sandro starts to open the door. Immediately he is hit by a bad aura. Thoughts of Medicare card and pregnancy challenges evaporate. In their place is a perplexing sense of impending evil. Lillian's face. The man behind her. Something is very, very wrong.

Sandro opens the door further. The derelict man steps forward to allow the door to open fully so Sandro can enter. The man says, 'Yeah mate, it's all right. Come in.' He is calm, unperturbed, doesn't bat an eyelid.

Sandro grasps Lillian's left arm and casually moves her away, places himself closest to the derro. Lillian experiences a relief of sorts. Her own electrically charged fear passes into the touch of Sandro's hand. But still she silently screams, go, go now.

On a chair just inside the 118 waiting room sits Tim. Tim has a touch of the likeable tough larrikin about him. At thirty-one, he is a large, cuddly sort of bloke who sports a beard and a warm, husky laugh. Tim is reading a magazine. He is oblivious to Steve, Lillian and Sandro. Cannot see them. Cannot hear them. The earliest act of a tragic scene is out of Tim's earshot, field of vision and interest.

Also oblivious to the rapidly unfolding drama, is Ingrid. A nurse on her tea break, Ingrid sits on the fire escape stairs abutting the small tea-room upstairs in 118. Extending from the rear of the clinic, the concrete steps of the fire escape are grey and cold. The backyard view is grey and cold too—concrete and metal chattels of walls, lane ways, cyclone fencing and cars. But it is a popular spot for the nursing staff. It can be a refreshing change from the sometimes-claustrophobic closeness of theatre and windowless recovery area. They are at least outside with the elements. The sky stretches out above them. The wind washes over their faces. If they're lucky, patches of sunshine fall softly around them. They can wind down for a bit with a chat, smoke and a cuppa.

Ingrid hugs a cup of coffee in both hands, and somehow manages to perch on the step in neat, ladylike fashion. Leslie, the charge nurse, squats casually on the step in front of Ingrid. One arm hangs limp toward the ground dangling a lit cigarette. The other arm reaches up to brush aside a wayward strand of her long blonde hair. The chatter between them mirrors their differing step-sitting styles. Ingrid's conversation is smiley and upbeat, polite and correct. Leslie's meanders along in a quick paced drawl, bumping into humorous idioms and unexpected expletives. But although their backgrounds and life-styles are quite different, they both believe fiercely in their work at the clinic. They both share the day-to-day hiccups and rewards of working in this unique women's health setting.

Two other nurses float in and out from the fire escape to the small staff kitchen, and in and out of the conversation. Their backgrounds and lifestyles are also quite disparate from their colleagues. But they too are dedicated to their work and to ensuring the wellbeing of the women in their care.

And so the four wind down today in their usual manner, unaware that on the level below them all hell is about to break loose.

At reception, Sandro now stands between Lillian and the unkempt man. Sandro is clear that this man is the source of the bad aura. But he is racing to catch up. What is going on? Who is he? What's this homeless person doing here? It is crystal clear that the derelict is the source of Lillian's fear and his own growing apprehension. But even Sandro is not prepared for what happens next.

Bad aura jolts into unadulterated terror. Adrenalin. Sharp. Stinging. This man has a gun. A semi-automatic rifle. High powered. This is no toy. It looms large. Everything else recedes into darkness. Oh, my God. Oh, my God.

The gunman raises it to his shoulder. Points it at a security guard.

No. No. No.

One shot.

Deliberate. Calculated. Cool.

No. No. Oh help me God.

Steve is knocked back. Crumpling at the knees. Weight on the filing cabinets. He's down. Eyes roll up. Blood from his mouth.

He's not dead. It's a shot to the arm. He can't be dead. But Lillian is seeing herself as a third person. She is in the eerie world of the psychologically dissociated state of mind. A normal but highly destabilising reaction to the shocking, overwhelming nature of what she has experienced. Nobody screams. Nobody does anything. Neither towards nor from. Time is suspended. An eternity spins in a split second.

Sandro knows otherwise. He hears her scream. He knows the truth. He sees it all. He knows he's gone. This is for real. This is for real.

Tiny sweet Tam. Standing at reception. Tam. Right here. Right now. She freezes in hot horror. She is immobilised. Stunned. Her body will not take direction. Steve is lying there. Bleeding. He has shot Steve. He has shot Steve dead. He has shot him. Steve.

Nostrils assaulted by pungent gunshot. Eardrums assaulted by the explosion of gunfire. Run. Run. The gunman is reloading the gun. I have to run. Run. Run. He is reloading. I'm next. Run. I'm next. Run.

Tam feels her body pushed into movement. It is painfully, frustratingly slow. Then it is a whirlwind of panicked speed. Down the long hallway. To the farthest room. There is a patient in front of her. Run. Run. Another shot. Shut the door. Lock the door. Tables. Chairs. Up against the door. The water cooler is too heavy. I'm not safe. It's not safe. Into the small storage room annexed to this one. Can't lock it. Push against it. Wait. Pray. Wait. Bite my hands with my teeth. Do I feel it? Am I alive? Pray. Wait. Ears ringing. Keep biting my hands. Am I alive?

He looks at his next victim. Composed. Unhurried. Re-cocks the rifle. Points it at Lillian's stomach. Dispassionate. Cold. You're next.

I'm next. Lillian waits for the impact of the bullet. Time stands still. There is nothing anyone can do. The inevitable will happen. I'm next. She is at the still point of the turning world. There is no time to reflect on her life and her loves. There is no what might have been or what has been. Sandro next to her is her only comfort. My darling, I'm next.

Lillian's next. You bastard.

Sandro jumps the gunman. His hands, his body, his whole being immerse themselves brutally into the gunman. You bastard. Sandro is consumed with the energising, life-hating, life-loving strength of anger. It is a fight for survival. The rifle swings wildly. Keep the gun up. Keep it pointing up.

The rifle discharges. Another mind-numbing, mind-piercing shot. Jolts Sandro's grasp. But the bullet mercifully finds only ceiling. Keep the gun up. Get him to let go his grip. Punch into him. Punch. Punch. He's strong. Oh God, so strong. Sandro pushes the gunman towards the wall. He's strong. Oh God. Help me.

Tucked just inside the waiting room, Tim's world is rudely and abruptly intruded upon. Via the open doorway between reception and the waiting room, Tim sees two men wrestling and hears bodies scuffling and souls straining. Tim has some sense that there has been a gunshot. Smoke and fibres hang in the air. But he is not scared. He is bloody annoyed. 'What the fuck's going on here. What are these two bloody idiots doing fighting in here.' Not naïve in the ways of male violence, and thinking the struggle is two blokes behaving badly, Tim intends to turf the pair of them out.

But something in Sandro's attitude compared with the gunman's makes it clear to Tim that Sandro is the good guy. Sandro is like Tim. And Sandro is in fear for his life. Sandro's intensity rapidly fuels the flickering flame of a weird awareness in Tim. This is no drunken or uncouth brawl. Here is a threatening presence. An enemy. A man who has a rifle. The gunman is still brandishing the rifle. Tim sees the rifle point in his direction. It is close. So close, he uses his hand and forearm in Tai Chi style to defensively brush the rifle aside. And then Tim pounces.

Seeing Tim come to their aid Lillian flees out the door. Get help. Get help. But she is no more out the door than she feels compelled to return. Push at the door from the outside. Three men weighing heavily against it from the inside. She cannot get past.

Turn. Run. A nightmare run for help. A nightmare of screams. Help.

Struggling with the gunman up against the venetian blinds of the reception door, Sandro now has an active, determined ally. Although Sandro is both big and strong, this grotty old man is surprisingly strong. Tim is a welcome participant.

Tim is a big man who knows how to throw a punch. He punches at the gunman's head. But the gunman tucks his head in to avoid further punches. Tim realises that if he continues to try to subdue the gunman by throwing punches at his head, Tim might accidentally hit his newly acquired mate, Sandro, who is on the other side of the gunman using his own muscle to subdue the gunman. The stubborn stamina of the gunman astonishes and troubles Tim. Tim punches at the gunman's ribs. But he finds that his hardest punches here are stymied by the gunman's ribcage. Aim for the kidneys. Thwack. Thwack. He can feel his fists penetrating deep into the gunman's body. Tim is in awe of the brute force of his own punches. He is in awe of his own savagery. Each punch is Tim's whole world. Each punch his whole being. There exists nothing else. There exists nothing beyond. Each punch is all that he is, all that he has been and all that he will be.

So why isn't the bastard falling. This old derro. This fucking bastard of a derro. I'm giving him all I've got. Tim feels panic for the first time. The gunman is inviolable. Neither he nor Sandro seem to be having any impact. Truth. Reality. Goodness. Godness. All are nought. But he's not giving up yet. He's never giving up. You bastard.

Smash the bastard's head. Tim grabs the gunman's head and slams it into the door again and again. At last. Thank God. The gunman is on the ground. The two younger men on top. All their weight. All their strength. Gasping for air. Sweating. Shaking. He's down. He's down. Hold him. Keep the fucking bastard down.

Throughout the clinic, the sound of gunshot assails the ears. The smell of gunshot assails the nostrils. In a split second, disbelief, confusion and fear startles into the decisive action of preserving life.

Lou's previous experience of violence insists that he instinctively run away from danger. You don't muck around. You get out of there. With patients in tow, he bolts out the back door. The mother, her 17-year old daughter and the daughter's boyfriend are amongst those taking Lou's lead. Arm around her daughter, hunched in trepidation, this mother cannot believe it. Not more. Not more for my daughter to deal with.

From their perch on the fire escape, Ingrid and her colleagues are surprised to see Lou and some patients dash out the clinic back door, scramble over the bonnets of cars and crouch behind them.

The quartet on the fire escape steps almost giggle at the unusual sight. 'What the…? Someone doing a runner?' asks Leslie with amazement. But why would Lou be leading the way? A loud muffled bang and they think that something very serious must be happening out the front.

'Oh, shit. Phone 23,' orders Leslie, but there is no answer from the small administrative office next to June's.

Ingrid decides to find out what is happening. She races down the internal 118 stairs towards the shots. She feels propelled towards danger. Ignores the trepidation at what she might find.

Within seconds she is back again. She is racing, furiously, gasping, her heart screaming. Oh my God. Ingrid still does not believe what her senses say is true. Her senses hit her like a physical blow. Gathered in one mighty punch to her stomach. She feels winded. Can't breath. Can't think. 'There's a man bleeding from the stomach.' Get the doctors. Get a doctor. Kathy!

At the sound of the shot, Kathy glances out of the staff lounge window into the street. Nothing there. Then she realises. The shot came from inside the clinic. Her response is immediate. She runs. Instinctively. Knowingly. Towards the shots. Towards danger. It is a well learnt, if self-denying, response. Kathy knows this scene. She's been there. Done that. Her time in hospital emergency in South Africa was filled with traumatic events, gunshots, requiring a quick, professional and unselfish response. And so she runs. She runs towards danger. As Ingrid races back up the 118 stairs, Kathy tears down the grand staircase in 116.

In the lab, the seated patient reacts so quickly that the others there later ponder that she must have known what had happened before it actually happened. She bolts out the back door, leaving her coat on the chair. Anais and her staff are still processing what is happening. What is happening?

In June's room, thoughts and ideas are abruptly interrupted by the noise of one gunshot, a scream, scuffling, yelling. Each sound cascades into the other, toppling over and into each other. A waterfall of violent sound and images sweeps over and through June. Over and through her patient. Hearts pound. Minds race. Lock the consulting room door. Dial 000. Another gunshot blasts.

The struggle continues in reception. For Sandro and Tim, the rifle is still a major concern. With their weight still on the gunman they both are trying to prise the rifle from his grasp. Finally. They have it. Drag it behind them away from his reach. Out of nowhere, another man appears, grabs the rifle. Sudden panic that this may be an accomplice evaporates rapidly. This man holds the gun up, out of harm's way, and runs it away from the scene. Runs back through the waiting area and across to 116.

Any relief this victory brings is quickly overtaken by other shocking emotions. For the first time, from his position on the floor, Tim sees the man slumped near the filing cabinets. Blood. Blood. It is a shocking realisation that imbues Tim with an overwhelming urge to assist this poor man. Go to his aid. But he must continue to hold the gunman down. Again, Sandro's attitude and focus becomes Tim's cue. The victim must be beyond help. He's dead, mate. We've got the shooter. We've got him. You fucking murdering bastard. You fucking killed him. Tim will keep the gunman down.

For a split-second Janice thinks the loud bang might be just a large box dropping on the floor or a car backfiring. 'Gee, that was loud,' she thinks. She jumps up in astonishment to lean over the switch desk and peer out through the glass of the front door. But she sees nothing untoward there. The smell makes it clear. It is a gunshot. A gunshot inside the clinic.

Janice's response is immediate and unthinking. She rounds the confines of the switch desk screaming at Susan and Tracey to get upstairs, yelling at other staff to stay upstairs and lock their doors, screaming to recovery staff to lock doors. She must protect staff and patients.

A man tears towards her holding a gun. There is absolutely no doubt now. Janice gets out of his way.

Tracey, who has been vacillating about going up the stairs, is now confronted with a crazed gunman running straight at her. For a ghastly split second, she freezes. The gunman is heading straight at her. She has no doubts that this is the gunman running away. He has the gun. It is pointed up. Gunman running away. Gun. Going out. Seems like a good idea to Trace. She races to the front door. Opens it wide. Out goes the man. Out goes the gun. Trace locks the door behind.

Susan, who had obediently started up the stairs, runs down again, just in time to see the man with the gun disappearing down the clinic path. Janice screams to Susan, 'Call the police. Call the police.' Then Janice runs towards danger.

Two gunshots in as many seconds. And June is through to emergency services with the second gunshot still ringing in her ears.

‘What sort of gun is it?’ he asks her.

‘Well, I don’t know. I’m locked in a room,’ replies June. ‘I can still hear scuffling. I’m locked in a room. I don’t know what is going on.’

The scuffling continues. The terror mounts. Locked in a room. Not knowing. Locked in a room. Just get here. Fast.

It is definitely a shot. That is definitely another. Anais herds her brood into the small lab next door which, unlike the large lab, can be locked. They lock and barricade the door. While Anais dials 000, they realise they are in a room filled with potentially dangerous chemicals. They have their own weapons for chemical warfare at hand. If the perpetrators get to them, they will use them. They dial 000. They hatch a scheme to protect themselves. They do not know.

Kathy and Janice race towards reception in unison. Kathy reaches Steve and, much to Tim’s relief, she clearly knows what she is doing medically and tries to resuscitate Steve. Janice takes in the scene. Steve bloodied and lifeless, but with Kathy attempting to revive him. Two men struggling with the gunman. Janice shouts encouragement, ‘Hold him down. Hold him down.’ Janice has no idea who these saviours are, but she is willing them with her heart to have the strength to keep the gunman down. They have him. Please. Please. Hold him. Please. Please. Don’t let there be an accomplice.

Between efforts to revive him, Kathy screams for Greg, ‘Get the oxyviva.’

Meanwhile, Janice is screaming for Greg to help Sandro and Tim, 'Greg. Greg. Help them.'

Greg's popularity at this juncture is not pleasant. The current climate of panic and high demand for a quick response from Greg by two different staff members in two contradictory ways—both highly urgent—is not a comfortable physical or emotional space to occupy.

'Get the oxyviva.'

'Help them hold him down.'

Susan is on switch. Dials 000. She is through quickly. Susan's beautifully correct receptionist lilt and diction rings out clear, if more harried and tremored than usual, 'This is the Fertility Control Clinic. There's been a shooting.'

But the operator's response doesn't seem right. She doesn't understand. The operator doesn't understand. In a desperate bid to convince the operator of the urgency of the situation, Susan adds with distinct emphasis, 'We are an abortion clinic.' Susan senses the inextricable link with what has occurred and our status as an abortion provider. Right to Life. America. Abortion. Shooting.

'Has anyone been hurt?'

Susan frantically relays the questions to Janice who screams back the answers as she scurries back and forth between 116 and 118. 'Steve's been shot. Steve's been shot. Hold him down. Hold him down.'

'Has someone got the gun?'

Susan extricates the answers from Janice's screaming directives.

'Hold him down. Hold him down. The police are on their way.'

'And what's your name? Susan, you've done a wonderful job.'

She is finished. She did it. Mingled with the terror and adrenalin is a small tingle of pride and relief.

Kate and a nurse tentatively open the connecting door between recovery and the post-operative lounge. Kate moves her patients from the lounge back through to recovery. Their attempt to barricade and lock doors is stymied. The connecting door can be locked, but the door into the hallway cannot be locked. Two men, who had been with their partners in the lounge, stand guard at the unlocked door. They don't know what is happening.

In recovery, Greg grabs the Oxyviva. 'Steve's been shot,' he says. And he is gone, leaving a wake of questions and fears behind him. Is Steve dead? Was it inside or outside? Is the gunman still on the rampage? Kate holds a vomit bag for a heaving patient and doesn't know. She doesn't know.

Tim is aware of other people coming in and out of the scene. The female doctor. The male doctor. A woman quickly locking doors, sensibly carrying out other tasks and screaming orders and encouragement.

And finally, as he continues to pin down the murdering bastard, Tim must concede what he does not wish to concede. He must bear the unbearable. The bloke by the filing cabinets is beyond help. There is nothing the doctors can do for him. There is nothing Tim can do. He is gone.

Janice finds a doctor's gown at reception and covers Steve's upper body, 'No need for staff to see that.'

Janice is in the zone. The zone of automatic survival instincts where others are her focus. Janice is everything and everywhere. But she is nothing and nowhere. She does not exist. Her feelings are nothing. Her safety is nothing. All that matters are the others. Their feelings. Their safety. Her covering of Steve's upper body is as much out of respect to Steve, as for her staff. It is not right for Steve to be seen like this. It is not right for others to see him like this. It is not right.

The quartet of nurses from upstairs bravely make their way down to recovery via the external, back entrance of 116. They feel strength in their community. They push their fears to one side. They know that there are sleeping patients in there. They feel compelled to help out. Walk back into the clinic to face an uncertain and dangerous situation. Not knowing.

Kate also stares her fears down to check on patients still in the dressing room area, whose preparations for theatre have been shockingly interrupted. She offers comfort and reassurance. A sense of control she does not feel but born from her professionalism. And Kate does not know.

Tim knows that they have the murdering bastard. He knows that the police have been called. But time is going at a snail's pace. Where's a bloody copper when you need one? At intervals, the gunman says that they're hurting him and can they ease up. But Tim and Sandro have no doubts about the need to contain him.

As time wears on, Tim twigs that the police may not realise that the siege is contained, the weapon removed, there is no danger. We've got the bastard and he's not getting out of this. Tim cannot even allow any thought of the alternative. Tim suggests that someone go outside to greet the police so that there is no misunderstanding about the status inside the clinic. Anything to hurry the coppers up. Where the hell are they? How long? How long has it been?

The police finally arrive.

The time it has taken a clock's second hand to move just ten times around the clock face has been psychologically bent into the infinite time warp of trauma. And within and beyond that infinity, a mere ten seconds of eternity. Ten seconds fighting for life. Ten seconds without end. Ten seconds where a lone gunman has stolen life and innocence. Ten seconds is all it took.

The arrival of the police finally and mercifully relieves Tim and Sandro of their protector role. Although this moment is what they have been aching for, it is hard to let go. Their physical grip on the gunman is intense. And the gunman's psychological grip on them is intense. When finally they release their hold, the relief is overwhelming. It tumbles out of them in spasms of physical shaking.

Despite her own shakiness, Tracey helps clean them up and takes Tim outside for a smoke, 'Come on Lovie, let's have a smoke,' she says. Tracey's bold jollying along is just what they need. She provides both strength and nurturance. She is a Godsend.

Susan heads for the consulting room where she left the young woman and her mother. Doing so, she glimpses Steve's body. Averts her gaze. Hurries on. It is all so close and confronting.

'Are you all right?' she asks through the closed consulting room door. They emerge shaken, but more concerned for Susan than themselves.

June and others emerge from their rooms. June checks the furthest consulting room. It is the room Kate usually uses to counsel.

'Kate?' June calls gently. But it is Tam. 'It's okay, Tammy. You can come out now. It's okay.'

6

Here is a place of disaffection
Time before and time after
In a dim light
T. S. ELIOT

But when I arrive that morning, it is not okay. And nor should it be. Normal human response to such a shocking and tragic aberration is to be 'not okay'. Abnormality. Numbness. Shock. Detachment. The absence of emotion, of feeling, of thought. The disengagement and discomfort of body. Bewilderment. With the event. With oneself. With it all.

And then in the following hours and days and weeks, the anger and fear and sadness. The sadness comes almost as a relief. Weighing heavy on one's heart, but with it some kind of deeper acceptance of the loss. Of life. Of innocence. Of our lives, and others' lives, as they had been.

But it is the anger, the fear and the questions, which taunt and tantrum, in unexpected abruptness or wearying persistence. The shooting is a brutal confrontation with death, rammed home by the violence of its eruption, its physical and emotional immediacy, and the inadvertent sighting of Steve's body by many staff in the aftermath of checking on clients and colleagues and providing witness statements within a cordoned off crime scene.

In the weeks and months to come, the fear is triggered by the most innocent and mundane of behaviours, noises, words. A persisting fear driving staff to check and recheck. Look and look again. Listen and then listen even more intently. Be alert. Be very alert.

Today, the huge police presence is reassuring. But still there is fear. There is fear despite the weird, wearying numbness.

I listen and watch and listen. I get caught up in phone calls and conversations and problems and questions and responses. I tighten my game plan. I try to be there. But mostly, I marvel at our staff. The more I hear, the more I see, the more I marvel. Their initial response—so varied, but all so right. I feel proud of them all. I am in awe of what they have been through and how they are dealing with it all.

Although my clinical training tells me it will be so, as their colleague I am bewildered by the harsh self-judgments which gradually emerge. I don't want them to go through this. They don't deserve it. I want them to feel as proud of themselves as I do. How can they possibly doubt that how they reacted, how they are behaving now, is anything less than courageous, caring, human and humane. I compare my own frazzled reaction to the morning's news and cannot help wonder—how I would have reacted? Not so well, I think. I marvel at our staff, my colleagues. How can they doubt themselves?

But already I hear their silences. And I know there will be the questioning, the self-doubt, the self-blame, the guilt for actions they did take, for actions they did not take. There will be the irrational 'what ifs' and the undoable 'could haves' and the impossible 'should haves'. There will be the frustrated anger at others who could have or should have or shouldn't have, or who should now or shouldn't now demand this or do this or not do this. But I see only a little of such anger. Staff may be tough on, and unforgiving of, themselves, but they seem to understand and appreciate their colleagues.

Already my questions and comments are geared towards sharing similarities and differences in staff response and reaction and feeling, and towards emphasising the normality and appropriateness of whatever an individual did and feels now.

Joan is startled, then admonishing herself. But it is too late. She sees it. What was a warm, kind person. Now cold. Lifeless. Soul less. Death.

Joan is a relative newcomer to the clinic, taking over the position of Clinic accountant after the death of our much loved and long time, elderly accountant. Now her role at the clinic is shaped by another death. While the first death was deeply sad but expected, the sadness of Steve's death is overwhelmed by the brutality of its unexpected execution.

A mature woman with the likeable hint of both motherly anxious concern and wisdom filtering through her voice and friendly attentiveness, at 10:20am this morning, Joan sits in her office almost directly above the 118 reception. She hears and smells the shots. She hears the scuffling, screams and yells. Finally stands on the grand staircase while a baffling unfamiliar world jostles around below her. At last police arrive.

Some time later, she is in her office upstairs again. Then down the narrow 118 stairs. Automatically. And it is too late. She sees him. She sees it. Maybe it is partially covered. But it is still a dead body. And it is a shock. Haunts her in nights to come. Death.

Other staff who accidentally catch sight of Steve's lifeless boot or trouser are similarly affected. After the shocking exhilaration of her emergency phone call, Susan returns unsteadily to 118. She stops abruptly. No further, she tells herself. Don't look, she tells herself. And she turns, focuses on the patient and companions she left just before it all happened. Goes to them. Blots out the sight of Steve's legs on the ground. Steve's legs.

For Tracey, it's Steve's boots. Imprinted on her brain. Those boots. All day. His boots. Greyness getting greyer.

For others it is much more than these fragments. It is the fragmented whole. The disintegrated whole which is Steve. But it is not Steve. Not now. No longer. Steve is gone now. At peace. This is a thing. An object. Devoid of life. The macabre vibration of death. Death which stalks staff. And Death which will stalk others.

Hours after the shooting, Joan sees from the edge of the waiting room, a ladder up to the reception ceiling. An overalled police worker fastidiously inspects the ceiling for spent bullets. Spent bullets in the ceiling. Spent bullets in the floor of Joan's office? Death takes another step closer. Joan sees its daunting omnipotence as she has never seen it before. Joan senses her own mortality as she has never sensed it before.

It is a morning of police needing statements, patients needing care, phone calls needing to be answered, phone calls to be made, plans to be put in place. Staff may be stunned, may take time out to call their loved ones, but they also continue to provide a service. They continue to care for our patients. They continue to provide support to each other. I feel so proud of them.

Susan and Kate are tag teaming at switch. Today it is a chore requiring considerable courage, fortitude and patience. Kate knows that she is there to answer incoming calls. She knows that the board will light up, it will emit a ringing sound, and it will do so whenever someone decides to call us. Kate knows this. She expects this. She has responded to this innocuous apparatus thousands of times. She is a competent receptionist. But increasing over the next couple of days, it is unexpected. It is unpredictable. Switch is jolting and threatening. The sudden ring. The flash of light. The flash of fear it triggers within her. The adrenaline surges which will not becalm. Today, the numbness and detachment of shock buffers Kate somewhat from a switchboard whose demands on her are already foreign and unsettling. It is wearying. Kate's complexion is greying. Her green eyes are translucent. Is she disappearing?

Calls to us are many. Kate has her set responses. One for the media. One for concerned well-wishers. One for well-wishers we know well. Another for unbalanced people who are taking this opportunity to taunt us. And amongst all of these, the usual calls for medical appointments from people not yet aware of what has occurred, or from people whose own crises wait for nothing and no one. 'Fertility Control Clinic. How may I help you?'

The door at switch swings open. Again. Because the crime scene is next door, the 116 door at switch is the only access in and out. It is busily open and shut. A parade of people, some in police uniform, some not. In and out. Some women, some men. In and out. Some clean shaven, some with moustaches and beards. Some carrying equipment, some empty-handed. In and out. It is expected and continual. Plain clothes police, uniformed police. She knows we are safe. But for Kate, each is sudden. Unexpected. Kate is jolted again. Recovers again.

Over the next few days, that door is a huge blowhole, blasting in on Kate unpredictably, carrying with it people unknown, waves of harsh, unwanted feelings washing over her. Then it recedes. Relief and quiet in its withdrawal. But knowing it will come again. Carrying who knows what. Each person enters in this way and leaps at her head on. Her sense of self-preservation triggered. High alert. Brace yourself. Who are you? Are you a threat? Are you a shooter? I don't think I can do this. Why am I doing this? Why do I have to do this?

Melbourne, 1960

She is twenty and single. Intelligent. Attractive. Hardworking. Dreams. Ambitions.

And pregnant.

Her heart pounds. Her breath catches in her throat. Surely she might die.

She sits in the back seat. He in the front. Quiet. Except for the whir of the engine. The drumming echo of her heartbeat. Surely he must hear it. Surely her heart will leap from her body. Surely it will explode.

She caught the right train. Got off at the right station. Searched the faces. Searched for a sign. But he found her. As she had been told.

'Where's the money?' he said. Nothing else as greeting he said.

Money exchanged like it was loose change. Not the six months' pay that it was.

'Put this on,' he said.

And as she seated herself in the back seat, she did.

Now, she loses track of time. Finally the car lurches around a bend, onto gravel. And it stops.

'Get out,' he says.

'Watch the step,' he says.

'Now to your left,' he says.

She smells antiseptic and dampness, and some other smell she cannot name. She hears a distant radio, senses another person in the room. Her heartbeat is deafening now. Surely she will die.

He handles her now. Sits her down. Then lies her down.

'It won't take long,' he says.

'Relax now,' he says.

And she tries to shut out everything. Everything but prayer. Please don't let me die. Please don't let me die. And she finally stops trying to see. Trying to guess. Trying to make sense of it all.

She awakes in the car. Or is she awake? She feels woozy, uncomfortable. Is she still dreaming? Was it all a terrible nightmare? She can't see, though she is sure now she is awake. Why can't she see? What is this pressure around her head? Shaking fingers to her head. Touches the fabric where skin, eyebrows and eyes should be. And she remembers. The blindfold. The blindfold is still on. The blindfold he told her to wear when first she entered the car. And she removes her hands from her face. Leaves the blackness in place. Like a good little girl. And she knows nothing. Is it over? Is she okay? Where is she?

She feels dampness and padding between her legs. And an aching, thumping deadness in her stomach, too frequently interrupted by a more piercing, shooting pain. She hates the jolts of the car. She begins to sob. Snuffling. Quietly. Not deeply and loudly as she wishes she could. She knows her nightmare is not yet over. She has a sense that it is only just beginning.

'We'll be at the station soon,' he says.

'Take these when you get home,' he says. And with one hand still on the steering wheel he reaches backwards with the other to her, half sitting half lying in the back seat. Lets a small brown paper bag drop in her lap.

She is shaking all over now. An uncontrolled shiver. She feels the tears welling up. Bursting to get out. The shame. The fear. The disgust that this man has touched her so. The violation.

But she is a good girl. She must not make a fuss. Besides she knows that she is one of the lucky ones. Her friend said he had been taught by his aunt, a midwife. He had access to anaesthetic—of sorts. She would be safe with him—maybe. She would not die with him. She would still be able to have children—she prayed.

She leans into the corner of the train carriage now, where the window meets the wall. She shrinks. Shrinks into the window. She makes herself invisible. Please nobody look at me. Please nobody know. Please.

It seems an eternity. She has enough money to get a taxi all the way home. 'I have the flu, I think,' she rehearses. 'And the curse has hit me hard today. I'll just go to bed,' she rehearses.

And her rehearsals are buffeted and strangled by her fears and her dreams. Will I be punished for ever? Will I ever find love? What else could I do? And she stifles her tears. Don't see me. Don't look at me. Don't know.

At some time, her faking of normality, her fears and shame and disgust, are taken over by anger. She finds strength and direction in her anger. She suffers the unbearable and unspeakable. No man ever has to go through this. No woman ever should. Men make the laws. I don't deserve this. No one deserves this.

Olive grows into a mature and wise woman. She becomes a politician. She works hard to make a difference. And she does. She is a fighter. And she never forgets.

Tragically she is struck down by a car. It is before her time. Many mourn her loss. She is time before and time after. We need her wisdom. We need her fight.

So, Kate sits at switch. Kate fights on. Today and the next. She is gutsing it out. She feels misunderstood, unappreciated. We take her courage for granted. We don't realise. There is too much going on. Kate is a soldier, fighting the good fight. And each staff member toughs it out in their own way. Today. Tomorrow. And for weeks to come.

In the near future only a couple of staff members will leave. Nearly all of us will stay. We know what we do and why we do it. No matter the trauma of the day and its shocking impact. Today staff still have patients to care for.

Natalie, a feisty, tousle-haired woman from interstate, is recovering from theatre this morning. She is keen to get back to her motel but we can't reach her partner. Another woman is ready to leave, but we cannot raise her husband who has their one-year-old baby in tow. Another is in a similar situation. Questions hanging over whether their partners have been caught up in it all. Are they being questioned by police now? Why don't they turn their phones on? How do we contact them? And how do we get the patients out of the clinic without the media invading their privacy?

'I don't care, I'll go out the front. Stuff 'em,' says feisty Natalie.

Others are not so sure. They are not so sure they want to be caught on the evening news. They know this is headline stuff. They know the media continues to camp out the front. But these patients are involved in private, personal matters. They don't particularly want to be on prime-time TV.

Out to the car park with a detective to suss out alternative 'escape routes' for our patients. It all seems so ridiculous, like the Keystone Cops or a French farce, if it were not so real and not so wrong.

Eventually, our patients are all collected by family and friends—all bar one who remains in need of medical care, and whose partner cannot be roused by phone. The rest head back to their own worlds. A day which was to be challenging enough, now knocks them further from their comfort zones. Perhaps for some, into the glare of notoriety. Perhaps the glare of embarrassment and shame. Perhaps of pride and relief. Or perhaps of psychological trauma.

Happily, most of the patients seem relatively untouched. They comment on the professionalism of the staff, the reassurance garnered from observing staff calmly and quickly taking sensible safety precautions which impress as routine and well-rehearsed. Their position and status in 116 appears to have provided them with a legitimate dependent passivity as a patient, and a psychological and geographic distance. Their patient position has afforded them a protective buffer to the morning's tragedy.

The morning wears on in its slow, frantic greyness. Witness statements. Phone calls. Plans. Discussion. Flowers. Cards. E-mails. Media requests. Patients. Partners. Patience. Fatigue.

It seems the news moves speedily, seismic shock waves emanating far from the epicentre. For some the news reactivates past traumas, or triggers fears of potential traumas. In the days to come, critical incident stress management experts are called in to other workplaces, specifically for the purpose of assisting staff deal with the issues raised for them by the shooting at our clinic. In the days to come, individuals we do not know lose sleep, hide away, check and recheck, and finally renew contact with their psychologist or psychiatrist. Perhaps even some anti-choice protesters might be prompted to rethink their role, their tactics. We can only hope.

Two police officers at the door. 'May we come in?'

'We are sorry to have to tell you that Steven has been killed.'

The world closes in. She does not know what she does. How she responds. It cannot be. It's not true. It is a nightmare from which she must surely wake.

How do you tell a loved one such shocking news? June is quietly appalled. There is no way to tell. How can you tell Steve's Mum? Steve's father died only weeks before. Shirley Rogers was widowed just weeks ago. And now this. What can we do? We want and need to do something. We should be doing something now.

And what of Steve's wife? His children? Although Steve and Sue had not tied the knot, Steve always referred to Sue as his wife. June knows that Sue would have been expecting him home. May have started to worry about where he is. What can we do for Sue? What of Steve's children? We want and need to do something. Shouldn't we be doing something?

Steve's job was to protect us. And now he has died carrying out that job. The people he loved, and the people who loved him. Helplessness. Empty empathy. Unanswerable questions.

In the days to come, June's experience with death and grieving families proves invaluable. Even today, she twigs to a possible family estrangement, and she is right. She is careful in her contact with Sue and Shirley. Ensures that she communicates fully to both. Makes no assumptions about any shared intimacy between them. But fortunately, her insight makes her a solid support for both Sue and Shirley for some time to come. Even while June carries a heavy burden at the clinic, ensuring we keep going, ensuring we still look after our clientele, ensuring she is there to listen to staff, even then, June is there for Sue and Shirley. Eventually, on separate occasions, Sue and Shirley come into the clinic. They are greeted with gentleness, concern, a ready sympathetic ear and thoughtful answers to the questions they pose. June, Janice and Lou are outstanding in their capacity to meet the grief of these women who loved Steve. We do what we can to contribute to their healing.

Our heroes and their loved ones. One might think that such heroism would sit proudly on a person's shoulders. A person's status and self-esteem enhanced. Sadly, not likely. At least not for some time. For some never.

Our heroes are first and foremost primary victims of a trauma. The self-doubts, what ifs, should haves, mortality, can become obsessions intruding mercilessly on body and soul. They have stood on solid ground only to find themselves at the mercy of Poseidon. The finger of the unknown, the unseeable, the incomprehensible, and the powerful. Its finger extending, targeting their world, their loved ones and themselves. Finger points at the solid ground. Ejects the mythical lightening bolt. Jolts the earth into spasms of terrible trembling. What they thought solid is disintegrating. Struggling to hold balance now. Nothing to hold on to. The trembling turns to earth quaking ruptures. Straddling cracks now. Deepening into crevasses. Which way to jump? How to escape? The world's dormant chaos let loose. Spiralling down into that blackness. Facing the demons. Questions, fears, doubts. Repeating in body and mind. Unrelenting. Safety and life direction betrayed. Sense of self both sharpened and vapid. For now.

For us now, they are wonderful, larger than life human beings who take our breath away. They take over our imagination, our lives and thoughts today, and for months to come. Our debt to them merely highlights the inadequacy of words. And yet words are all we have to thank them. And we will thank them. We must thank them.

Detective Senior Sergeant Lucio Rovis sits in the admissions office, the intimate embrace of phone in hand to face. We know he is dealing with a multitude of practical tasks and emotional people. He is our source of information and reassurance. I seek Lucio's advice about whether they have found out anything yet about the gunman. Who he is. Why he did it. Why he targeted Steve. Or why he targeted us. Who are his associates. I want something, anything which might be helpful to staff.

The gunman is not talking, reports Lucio. Will not even give his name. We know nothing about him. We know nothing of his motives. We know nothing of his associates. But we'll find out, says Lucio. The most important thing is, 'we've got him'.

So we are okay. We are safe. Perhaps, we think. We are safe.

They find the shooter's bag two hours after. An armoury of ammunition which is substantial. Enough flammable material and accessories to turn the clinic and all inside into a pile of ash.

The discovery is mortifying in its unambiguous intent. He had not come to take out one or two people. He had come to do the whole place.

Everything.

Everyone.

It is Christmas 2000. In a small New South Wales town, he arrives for Christmas with his family.

His mother died in the 1980s. His father is alone now and troubled by dementia. He has five adult siblings, and he came into the world of this Catholic, farming family at Bathurst, on 1 January 1954, although the Truth that now illuminates his path tells him that his 'birth' occurred nine months earlier—at conception. Living and being schooled in various locations, he was educated to the age of sixteen, up to Year 10, at Catholic schools. In his 1970 De La Salle Catholic High School yearbook there is a photo of him at 16, wearing blazer and tie, sitting proudly in the front row of the class photo, beaming at the camera. The epitaph, probably then alluding to a juvenile preoccupation with passing wind, but now with chilling prescience, says, 'Silent but deadly.'

He finally left the family home when he was in his early twenties and lived for fourteen or so years in Brisbane, working in factories before returning to the area of his birth to become the local hermit. He has never been in trouble with the law. To his family he is a misunderstood loner, a directionless drifter who is self-absorbed, eccentric, socially inept. He has not a clue about how to dress. He looks so dishevelled, but they guess healthy enough. They have not an inkling that the man they knew as a boy, as a babe, the man they know as a son and brother, is on the path to becoming a murderer. And but for the fickle hand of fate and the courage of others, would see him become a mass murderer.

It has been twelve years since he divorced the world of men and women. But it is incomplete. In fact it cannot ever be truly severed. And now he does not want it to be. In the past, it besieged him mentally. He knew it. He was tortured and ostracised. But he has turned the tables. Turned the tables so completely, they won't know what's hit 'em.

Like all the great thinkers, his ruminations take him in undreamed of directions—glorious, wonderful schemes. His thinking and dedication is testimony to his sympathies for the young who are so vulnerable to the lies and seductive lures. He mulls it all over. How it happens. How to stop it. The cancer plague created by the tobacco companies. The poison they peddle to the young. Those greedy, murderin', multinational bastards.

He thinks and reads, researches, works and writes.

But then it comes to nought. Although he does not see it, he stills needs the validation of others. There is nothing and no one out there to fan the flames of his endeavour and disdain. But what he does come across excites him more than the tobacco murderers. His ideas find inspiration from afar. He discovers others who think like him. They extend his ideas. Instruct him. Encourage him to keep going. And so he develops his manifesto. His enlightenment extends beyond theirs now. It is time for him to enlighten them. They will welcome his ideas. He is the great teacher now. His ideas are connecting with action he can affect.

But he must be meticulous. And he is. He is obsessive in his determination and in his research exploring the outrageous, sewerage of mankind and getting to know the enemy intimately. Better than it knows itself. To thine own self be true and know thine enemy. The bastards.

The minute detail and obsessive ritual he must now impose upon himself. He must not leave a trail. No connection. He will travel far but not be seen. He must not exist, and he will not. Not even a fingerprint. Soon it will be time to don gloves—for everything. He will not leave a trace. Just another fragment of his obsessively orchestrated and calculated plan which he is patiently bringing to fruition. He knows he is of superior intellect and he knows his methodical approach leaves nothing to chance. He is moving closer to being a true crusader for the innocent. What a merry dance he'll lead 'em. Not a bloody trace of him anywhere. He will come like the wind and leave like a ghost. The man who does not need man or woman. The man who is better than them all. They won't know what's hit 'em. Ha!

But for now, he is with his family. Christmas. The ritual time of giving and receiving, of love, holiness and peace on Earth.

The flash of the camera triggers a fleeting anxiety quickly swamped by his indignant anger. He has invested so much to ensure his anonymity. Bloody hell woman what are you doin'? He is a man of ruthless action. This cannot happen. So it will not happen. He is up and at 'em. Grabs the camera. How do you open the bloody thing? Yes. Rip the black entrails from its insides.

Even in his world where he has trouble reading the meanings comprising social transaction, he is aware that his action has startled her. A hint of fear in her eyes. But it is everything and nothing. Nothing must get in his way and nothing will. They do not realise what is at stake.

But they will. Oh they will. And they will praise Him. They will praise His name.

7

Thus with the Dead as with the living, What?
And Why? So ready, but the Wherefor Not
RUBAIYAT OF OMAR KHAYYAM

At the bag's initial discovery, police proceed with caution. The danger must be assessed accurately and then contained or defused. Worst case scenario would be a typical terrorist stratagem—following the successful foiling of one attack, there exists another attack, undetected, but coiled ready to spring. At first, police are concerned the bag may contain an explosive device.

Without arousing staff concern, police want all staff in one area, away from reception. For now, knowledge of the bag and its contents is restricted. It is disturbing information. Most staff are thankfully unaware. They are dealing with enough. This little extra gem of information will be communicated and dealt with at a time when it has been clarified, in a forum appropriate to staff needs and prior to media disclosure. That is, assuming we don't all hear about it sooner via a very big bang.

The timing of our proposed staff meeting coincides with police confining us all to the other side of the building. The police see the congregation of staff as a necessary safety precaution while they clarify the danger posed by the gunman's bag. Most of us congregate knowing that it is an important staff gathering and information session. Time for our individual experiences to come together to find validation and support. A healing process can start by harnessing the powerfully reassuring experience of coming together and sharing knowledge and gaining knowledge both about what happened and what is happening, what is likely to happen, and what we will be putting in place to ensure staff are supported through this aberrant and tragic event. We are a close-knit group usually. I am optimistic about our capacity to comfort and bolster each other.

But there is an urgent, aching chasm for staff. Why? Why did it happen? Why Steve? Was Steve his target? Or were we his main target? Why us? Why here? Who is he? Why did he do it? Had he been to our clinic before? Is he working alone? Are we still in danger?

The answers to such questions are often crucial in people reconciling themselves to a trauma. Like healthy human beings, we want to understand why this violation occurred. We need to understand the why's. We need the reality, no matter how frightening, to overcome the imagined, which is usually even more frightening. We need the perspective of reality to overcome the self-centred psychological torment of self-doubt, self-blame, guilt, anger, fear, grief.

It is just three hours since Steve was shot and killed. A lone gunman disarmed, handcuffed, removed and questioned. In other violent incidents, substantial information can be available in this time frame, and it can be shared with victims to help them make at least some sense of it all.

But not here. The gunman is not talking. Not telling even his name. He has no documents. His fingerprints do not match any in the police data bank. He is a nobody. He has no identity, no associates, no motive, not even a home. He does not exist. He is a ghastly spectre who has passed through our lives in an insidious and malicious form. And he will continue to pass through people and space and time. The shivering of evil passes disturbingly through us, but also through others. As this day and the subsequent days progress, we will see the troubling impact of not knowing. It will feed our insecurities and fury.

The day after Steve's murder, Tuesday 17 July, Steve's mother makes a public appeal for knowledge about the identity of this man who killed her son, and the police take the unprecedented step of publicising the gunman's photo. In the photo he has a goatee beard and wears jeans, a flannelette shirt and shabby work boots. He is dubbed Mr X by the media and referred to as John Doe and Unknown at his Melbourne Magistrates Court appearance that day. Over the next two days, police receive more than 40 calls in response to the publicity. But it will be days before the police have any inkling and weeks before they make a definite ID.

In the meantime, the killer continues to be as passively uncooperative as he can. He continues to delay and flout the authority of our legal system and shows callous disregard for the people most in need of the knowledge only he has. We are reassured that it makes little difference to the legal process or the case being built against him. But it makes a significant difference to the way we, and others, reconcile ourselves to the tragedy.

So now, and for weeks to come, I have nothing to share with staff in the way of reality of motive. Why? Why this shocking deed? Why kill Steve? I have nothing to help staff make sense of it all. Nothing to help staff regain some sense of safety and sanity.

We are extremely fortunate and eternally grateful that the perpetrator has been captured and that we are safe. For now. We hope.

His physical being is captured. But without an identity, a motive, he is free to haunt us and others. We want to know more than this.

Theories will run hot and not be helpful. Fears will continue around accomplices, copy-cats, involvement of anti-choice groups, links with violent anti-choice organisations overseas. Staff members will rack their brains about men who have accompanied patients recently as well as months ago. They will recollect the protesters out the front—the regulars and the unfamiliar. They will remember visits by protesters harking from overseas. But still we will not know.

The reality is that our questions will never be fully answered anyway. We will never fully understand how and why a person could carry out such an unspeakable deed. Our focus now must be on sharing, supporting, validating and educating ourselves about the normality of our reactions then, now and in the future, and on being reassured that assistance is at hand.

It is 1.30pm, just three hours after the shooting death of our security guard. In the patient lounge, we move furniture so that chairs and sofas hug the walls to create a large circle for staff. Lou, Janice and Greg stand near the door. Throughout, Lou or Janice disappear briefly to deal with clinic business, then return. The rest of the staff sits snugly together. This includes a couple of staff members who, on this their day off, hear the news and come into the clinic.

I hope that my introductory comments invite staff sharing, whether that be to listen, to talk, or to ponder. Some are keen to talk. Others to listen. Most sit respectfully, still numb, detached, or shivering. I do not want too much detail. I do not want staff feeling that they have to speak. I do encourage accounts from those who I know have already spoken of their experience to others, and who have a unique knowledge of what happened which others will likely find helpful.

Whenever I can, however I can, I emphasise three messages. First, that people reacted differently at the time, and however they reacted was the right way for them and was understandable and positive. Running to the shots, running away from the shots, locking and barricading, not being sure what to do—all are valid. Second, there will also be variability in how they are reacting and feeling now and in the next few days. Whether they feel nothing, or feel highly distressed, whether they sleep like a log, or have difficulty sleeping, no matter how much distress is present or absent, theirs is a normal reaction to an abnormal situation. And third, we have a solid game plan to optimise staff safety, recovery and future wellbeing.

I pass out photocopies of a notice provided by Senior Detective Sergeant Rovis. It is on official Victoria Police letterhead.

Crime Department
Homicide Squad CIB
412 St Kilda Road
Melbourne 3004
Victoria, Australia

RE: INCIDENT IN EAST MELBOURNE ON 16/07/2001

Your assistance this morning is greatly appreciated. The investigation into this matter, and any subsequent Court proceedings, will continue for quite some time.

The Police Officer in charge of this investigation is Detective Senior Sergeant Lucio ROVIS of the Homicide Squad. If at any time you have queries, or further information, you can contact the Homicide Squad [phone number provided].

Victoria Police also have a Victim Advisory Unit which can be of assistance in providing counselling and other services to assist any person who may feel traumatised by having been involved in this incident. For queries of this nature please contact Scott at the Victim Advisory Unit or alternatively Scott can be contacted 24 hours a day by pager [phone numbers provided].

My name and home number are scrawled at the bottom. I emphasise that this is an open invitation for anyone to contact me tonight, at any time, or over the next few days. That night I sleep with the phone next to my bed.

I announce that we will be bringing in external psychologists. Tomorrow I will have details about this.

It is after 2:30pm by now, when Tam appears at the staff meeting after providing a statement to police. She has been through an ordeal we cannot even imagine. Not just her witnessing of the shooting, fleeing for her life. But also the shocking confusion afterwards. The surreal unfamiliarity. The misreading of cues. The shuddering seconds when Tam thought she was to be transported to police headquarters in the same car as the gunman, with the gunman. The gunman staring at her from the police car. Her dreadful reliving of the tragic drama during her police interview. And finally, in what can take other primary victims weeks or years to accomplish, Tam returns to the scene of a brutal murder. A cold blooded, brutal murder carried out just inches from her. The victim a person she knew and liked.

We all want to rally to comfort her. Gently. Not too fussy. She is visibly shaking, as are many of us. The whole experience has chilled us to the bone, made us sick to our stomach, we cannot digest what has happened. Our estrangement from our bodies feeds back into the emotional shock and exhaustion which perpetuates this weird bodily discomfort. Poor sweet Tam is tired and empty. Her body is foreign to her. But here she is.

Kate gives Tam a glass of water. Susan tells Tam a friend rang for her and her friend is coming to pick her up to take her home. I get Tam a copy of the information sheet with my home number on it. 'Oh, I thought I lost you,' a doctor says, 'What would I do without you.' Our words and actions try to envelop her with warmth and safety.

Now, Tam has to leave. She is meeting her friend two blocks down, and her friend will take her home. This vulnerable, but brave, young woman. Already she has returned to the clinic where demons can jump out at her at any time. But hopefully she feels the warmth of concerned friends, the compassion of this place. Vicki, one of our counsellors, and sensibly alert and sensitive, volunteers to escort Tam to her friend's waiting car. Vicki, like me, was not in at the time of the shooting, but came in quickly afterwards. Vicki, like me, is part of all this too, and Vicki, like me, can do things that others cannot.

I decide to go with Tam and Vicki too. This is the first time I have seen Tam since it all happened. It is not the way the meeting is meant to end, but it can't be helped. There might be positives in staff being able to wind down now all together more informally. I must accompany Tam. It is five past midnight on this Monday afternoon at three o'clock.

As we walk out the back door, through the car park, down a back lane and then onto the street, we avoid any media. Tam is understandably shaky, physically off balance and seemingly unaware of traffic. Vicki and I hold her either side gently, guiding her, stopping at times to avoid cars, gutters and other hazards to which Tam is not attuned. As we walk, Tam talks a little about her ordeal, growing more confident about speaking as we go. And Vicki and I are good listeners—that and being able to provide clear validation of her feelings and experience. That is what we do. I encourage her to see her local doctor tonight. Apart from everything else, Tam needs to have her ears checked. They have been ringing since the gunshots.

She is safely to her friend's car. We repeat various instructions to her friend, not sure that Tam has taken them in—see her doctor, my number is on the sheet, don't hesitate to call. Sweet Tam. She is so polite, smiling gratefully. 'You all so nice to me.' We fear for her battle against the demons.

When I return to the clinic, the nursing, lab and most other staff have left. I feel uncomfortable about the unfinished staff gathering. I worry about all that was not said. I worry that I should have done better for our staff. But it is early days. I'm working on our game plan.

Like the morning, the rest of the afternoon is another whirl of fragmented conversations, visual and auditory snapshots all worn down by a grey weariness.

Two suited detectives hunch over the coffee table in the recovery lounge, munching on salad sandwiches—a very late lunch. They are in detective mode. They have a crime to piece together. While they chew on their sandwiches, they also chew over what they know, what they need to know, and how they're going to find out. They toss around theories about motive, planning, associations. Who the hell he is.

Clearly Steve was not the primary target. The shooter had waited until he thought Steve had left for the day. And the contents of the shooter's bag makes it crystal clear that the entire Clinic was his target. Mass murder was his goal.

Male clientele with a vendetta? Do staff recall any? The shooter's possible links with anti-choice groups and with our own protesters is a logical avenue of enquiry to pursue too. June, Janice, Lou and others are a mine of information. They know them all by appearance, name, personality, behaviour, and have some sense of how long they've been around. They dig out old photos and more recent photos, old pamphlets, website addresses.

I feel I can be of no help in this regard. I don't know the protesters. I go out of my way not to know them. I don't look at them. I don't listen to them. I make them invisible.

I am walking back to the clinic from Libby and David's café with my cappuccino. It is about 100 metres walk there, but sometimes walking back it grows to 1000 metres. I am wearing black trousers with a red jacket. I look nonchalant, I think. Just another morning on Wellington Parade. I take in the trees. We're so lucky in Melbourne with our tree-lined streetscapes. Yep. A protester is coming my way. Guess at the weather—wonderfully changeable. Notice a car coming out of a basement car park. Yep. Here she is. There's the building where Simmo used to work. She sidles up beside me. She is walking along with me now. There might be a hair's breadth between us. I look in the travel agent's window at Balmy Phuket… Sizzling Spain. 'You are wearing the colour of the blood you spill.' Oh, look a little bird picks up a crumb from the pavement. 'You are wearing the red of the blood of the precious children you murder.' I notice a drop of coffee bubbling out of the takeaway plastic top. 'Don't kill the babies.' I wipe the coffee drop with my thumb as it slides down the cup towards my hand. 'Don't kill the precious children. Save the precious infants.' Ah, there is Steve. 'You're the last of the few doing the dirty work.' Steve sees me and gives me a grin. I see the glint of a cross hanging around her neck. I walk past the others now. Two men and another woman. They are standing on the footpath facing the clinic. Their heads are bent in prayer. Bibles are open in their hands. They babble on. As I pass they join in the insulting entreaties. 'Save the little children. Do not go in there. Do not murder the children. Call on Jesus' name….'

Some days, they seem to be yelling a great deal. Some days there are others yelling back. They might be our patients, partners of our patients, or other people in the neighbourhood who have had enough. It can be rather disconcerting in the middle of a consultation when a barrage of apparently loud-mouthed lunacy carries into my room from the front of the clinic.

Other days, at least for some of their time, they do not accost me or others. We ordinary folk just going about our own business. Some days they just stand in their spot on the footpath, facing the clinic gate, standing quietly, praying. They leave the intimidation to their macabre posters, their ludicrous literature, their very presence. Perhaps they are after all harmless. Perhaps they are even kind, considerate people with families of their own. Just insensitive to the rights and feelings of anyone who walks past our clinic, attends our clinic, or works at our clinic. They are mostly neatly dressed, conservative, middle-aged or elderly. Sometimes they even bring a small child along—a sign of their parental and humane priorities perhaps. As a clinical psychologist who has worked with children extensively, not what I would call a very good parenting move. They are showing their children that bullying is acceptable, laudable. They misinterpret Jesus' compassionate teaching to suit their cause, give themselves respectability, and threaten others. And their children take it all in.

Even if they spend time quietly, their posters and their misinformation are obscene and dangerous, and their quiet time just makes their vilification and intrusions all the more unpredictable and offensive. Today, at this time, I am clearly fair game. This one, younger, more casual in dress, has decided to up the anti a notch, as they sometimes do. If I'm feeling uncomfortable and intimidated, just how bad is it for the women and their families who consult us? I wonder why this does not fit the definition of stalking.

But I don't see her. I don't hear her. I don't see them. I don't hear them. It's just another day popping out for a coffee. You might run into a person accusing you of being a murderer and trying to intimidate you from entering your place of work. But, I'm just grabbing a coffee. As you do. 'G'day, Steve.' She is still beside me right to the gate. 'Not a bad day, eh? You might get a spot of sunshine here today.'

Then I am inside. I haven't seen them. I haven't heard them. They don't exist.

Gina is fed up with them. She is a ball of cheeky anger. She pushes her way through the protesters, her flaming hair flowing in her wake. 'Get out of my way. Pregnant woman coming through.' Her belly protrudes round and huge. She looks almost ready to deliver. She nurses it proudly with her two arms. 'Pregnant woman coming through. Get out of my way.' And she enters the clinic.

Five minutes later and Gina leaves the clinic the same way. Out the front door, down the path and through the front gate. Struts past the protesters again. 'Ooh that's better,' she sighs. Pats her flattened tummy where the plump cushion had been.

Lou strolls out to the protesters. 'Hey, Dave. Is your wife pregnant?'

'None of your business,' comes the indignant reply.

'Exactly,' says Lou. And seeing that the penny doesn't drop, Lou adds, 'Just like it's no business of yours to know about the women coming here.'

I don't feel quite as cowardly knowing that even Kate usually will not venture out alone if the protesters are there. She hates that they intimidate her so, too. But it is the afternoon of the day Steve is killed, and the protesters are long gone.

Kate goes out the front and picks up a bunch of flowers left there, brings them back to switch. 'Here's another,' she says, bringing the simple bouquet to her nose. 'Read the card,' she says sadly. 'It's so lovely.' Already, flowers and letters and cards arrive at the clinic, or are just left outside on the blue stone steps, at Steve's post. The latter seem the most poignant. It all continues for days.

Susan at switch says, 'Thank you very much. I'll pass your condolences on.'

June in the admissions room checks on emails. I don't usually associate June with technology, but here she is. Her celebrant studies forced her to become computer literate. Amidst everything else, June takes on the job of responding to all the emails pouring into the clinic over the next few days. They come from the local area, interstate and overseas.

I go to and fro with bits and pieces, this and that. Endlessly. As the time goes on, there seems to be more to attend to. But I am used to life as a succession of interruptions. So used to it, that I am amazed, but very grateful, when my first phone call to Simon Brown-Greave's Occupational Services finds Simon available to take my call. A good omen. A better omen is that his reassuring voice on the other end of the phone line is a fragment of soothing colour midst the day's bleak grey. He takes the time to listen and to comment, offers helpful tips. When he asks when we would like someone to come in, I know I would like it to be tomorrow morning. He promises a colleague, the trauma manager. He thinks she will suit us and she will be here tomorrow at 10am, Tuesday 17 July.

A few phone calls later I am feeling very pleased with myself. I have managed to tee up an appointment for Tam with a Vietnamese speaking psychologist who deals with posttraumatic stress. Although Tam's English is excellent, being able to speak with someone about all this in her native tongue might have benefits.

Two days later I cancel this appointment. Tam says she would rather talk with me. Her friendships here, her attachment to us, are what facilitate her recovery. She will work through things here with us, with me and with our consultant.

Detective Senior Sergeant Rovis of the homicide squad is a reassuring and calm presence. Always welcoming of a question, he is never too busy for us. Still, I try to put off bothering him until I have a number of items to raise. I check what he thinks about us contacting our heroes Tim and Sandro and Brett—the young bloke who ran the rifle out of the clinic. How are they doing? What can we do for them? How can we thank them? We don't want to intrude. We don't want to aggravate their situation. Any suggestions about what might be best at this stage?

They're doing it pretty tough, he says. They'll need some time, he says. But a letter should be okay. We decide a formal, short letter of thanks might be appropriate for now. He provides me with names and contact details for our heroes. They will be recommended for a commendation, he says.

June finds out Steve's partner's address and his mother's so we can contact them too. I am starting to have some idea of the enormous workload ahead of us, but only an inkling. It is still only hours since the shooting. I make a note to contact every patient in person, by phone, tomorrow. Yes, I must contact all of them when I get in tomorrow, check they are okay. But the next day brings with it the reality of what has befallen us. In the midst of the increased workload, there is no way I can contact patients individually. A week later, the number of patients I have spoken to personally is very small. Hardly any have contacted us troubled by the shooting. We send out a letter to our patients:

> Dear Jane,
>
> We wish to apologise for any distress or inconvenience experienced by you and your family as a consequence of the tragic shooting death of our security guard, coinciding with your appointment here on Monday 16th July.
>
> We have been advised by the police that anyone seriously and adversely affected by this incident can contact Scott Garnett of the Victim's Advisory Unit.
>
> We thank you for your understanding in this matter.

At five o'clock the day of the shooting, Janice sits at switch, wan. Like most of us, she has not wanted to eat all day. Not many of us can stomach it. None of us can stomach this.

'Can I get you something to eat?' I ask.

'I just couldn't eat anything all day. You know just that nausea.'

'It might make you feel better. What about a cup of tea? Some dry bickies?'

'Well, OK,' she relents.

Ten minutes later, she seems a little revived, 'I do feel a bit better after that.'

It is around six o'clock in the evening. The three of us remaining—Lou, Janice, and me—are all wilting. We are just hanging on, hanging out at switch, when finally the coroner arrives. An unexpectedly extravagant vision of femininity—resplendent long blond hair and flamboyant red coat. A photographer accompanies her. Just as quickly she is gone, and Steve's body with her. The police cleaners never arrive. A police officer and our own clinic cleaner work to have the reception area ready for tomorrow's patients, remove the blood stains, remove the signs of Steve's murder.

We leave tonight not knowing. Who he is. Why he did it. Why us.

8

Men and bits of paper, whirled by the cold wind
That blows before and after time
T. S. ELIOT

She begins to walk briskly now. Hugging her bag to her chest, even though the strap holds it to her shoulder. Hunching over herself protectively, she dare not look around. She behaves like the small child in a game of hide and seek who hides by covering her own eyes or turning her own back on the seeker. If she cannot see the seeker, then nor can the seeker see her, says the normal egocentrism of childhood. If she does not look. If she keeps her back turned. Perhaps he will not see her. Perhaps he will no longer exist. Perhaps he will go away. Go away.

The blue stone lane way is uneven. She is relieved she wore her runners. Even so, she keeps tripping in and out of the stones. Her lack of physical balance further unsettles her now precarious mental balance. She is not even sure if this is the way. She hopes she is going the right way. She has to keep on—he is still there, right behind her. He is panting now, too. Panting between his crazed yells of murdered babies, the blood of the children, do not kill your child… The yells which seem to grow louder, more urgent. Why doesn't he leave me alone. Go away. 'Go away.'

She breaks into a run. His crazed stalking is one step away from assault. She is frightened, frantic now. What might he do?

He runs too. Still yelling. Still a threat.

Her breath comes in panicked gasps now. Where is the door? Let me in. 'Let me in!'

'By the time she got in the door she was hysterical. Absolutely hysterical. And can you blame her?' Janice is seething. Despite the trials of the previous day, Janice's spunk is unwavering. 'A single woman. Up a lane way. He's chasing and yelling at a lone woman. Alone in a lane way. The day after a murder for goodness sakes. Bloody hell. What do they think they are doing. The poor girl was hysterical. Hysterical.'

I can only agree that this is indeed madness. Sadly, it is not uncommon for protesters to stalk patients in this way. Whether it is up the cobbled lane way, 'accompanying' them to or from their car or mistakenly picking out women who are not patients at all but are just in the neighbourhood. Of course their stalking involves verbal harassment too. Apparently this is what the protesters call offering 'counselling'.

Today, this type of behaviour takes on an even more sinister quality. And it is absolutely unforgivable. Janice has been on to the police and our security firm. We will have three, not one, security guards this afternoon when police will no longer have a presence. We will continue to have three for many weeks. We will change security firms and we will complete the introduction of a video surveillance and buzzer entry security system within six weeks.

But for now, security remains a source of concern and anguish for staff. It goes way beyond the usual intimidation of the protesters. A simple duty of care is owed to our staff and our patients. Surely, at this time, of all times.

Janice is justifiably angry. 'We don't know who the guy is. We don't know whether he is in cahoots with the protesters, whether he has an accomplice, plan B, whatever. How can the police do their job when protesters are blocking access and a view of the clinic. And how can that madman of a protester do that to that poor woman?'

And I don't know.

It is the day after a murder. The day after our security guard was shot and killed in cold blood in the reception area of our clinic. The day after a lone gunman entered our clinic with enough ammunition and flammable material to kill everyone in it and leave the place a pile of ashes. The day after people displayed immeasurable bravery and fortitude, suffered untold terror, and now face personal challenges they wish they never had to face. And protesters, who claim that life is sacred, display no regard whatsoever for the lives of our staff, our patients or our neighbours.

As anyone who has any experience with traumatic events like yesterday's will tell you, and anyone with a modicum of common sense would work out, today the mood is one of overwhelming fear, exhaustion and a weird sense of warped reality. The adrenalin surges keep attacking like lethal pinpricks. Hypervigilance, hyperalertness, overactive imaginations and jumpy insecurity override all else.

Footfalls echo in the memory. At times they are deafening. Reception is of course a difficult station. Switch is also demanding. These spaces where sound and people intrude and startle. Staff needs constant reminders of the security measures in place, the vetting of clients before they enter. June, in her sensible mothering way says several times today, 'Today has to be the safest day ever. The day after a murder. Police everywhere. No one's going to try something today.' And we laugh and feel comforted by our bond together, even if we are not convinced she is right. And that bond keeps us going.

In the lab, Anais expresses all the fear uncensored, up front, in hushed or dramatic tones. Her staff peppers the conversation with quiet, short comments and embarrassed smiles. They are caught up in the 'whys' and 'what fors', the 'what ifs' and the fear. The coat left behind is a spooky sign of that woman's clear involvement in the crime? Perhaps she had come with the shooter? Perhaps they themselves had seen the shooter before? Had he been to the clinic before? Things usually not noticed are now focused on, feared. A door touched by the wind, signal an intruder. The shadow, or footstep, of a person passing by must be investigated.

In the days to come, the fear continues. What is reasonable, what is irrational is sometimes unclear. The man who comes to the 116 door, head to toe in black bikie gear, his face hidden behind an opaque helmet he does not remove. We do not let him in. He has some story about having lived here, wanting to visit. It is bizarre. We phone the police. His name does not match the bike registration. He is questioned. The security guard, concerned about a man sitting in a car outside the clinic for hours, alerts the police. Again the story is not straight forward. Our suspicions were worthy of checking.

I tear down the 116 staircase. It is Thursday morning. I'm bounding. I'm fleet footed with energy to spare. Two little pills last night, prescribed by Greg, and I am revived. I slept from 8:00pm last night to 4:00am this morning. And it feels so good. I was up at 4:00 am. Typing. Coffee. A brisk walk. Lunches. Washing. Goodbyes. And I'm in. The banister shudders in reply to my exuberance. I land with a thud at the bottom, 'Good morning.'

Tracey jumps two feet in the air. She is in alarm. The sudden impact. The shocking sudden impact. And I am apologising. How could I? What sort of a friend am I? What sort of a psychologist? I know switch can be hell on earth at the moment. 'I'm so sorry Tracey. I'm sorry.'

And so it goes on. The fear spills out into the everyday world away from the clinic.

She sits at the cafe table in the shopping mall. She is just one of many, sitting and sipping on a frothy coffee. Bags of shopping lean beside her chair, her handbag is slung over the back of the chair. It is a pleasant weariness she feels. She has enjoyed the distraction of window-shopping and bargain hunting. Now the relaxing replenishment of a cup of coffee, surrounded by bustling movement, colour and noise. She is safe in the luxury of the ordinary and the known.

But her awareness of what is around her starts to tilt. It is unexpected and unwanted. Her body signals danger. Heart pounds. Heat rises. Clammy skin. He looks a bit strange, she thinks. He is looking at me, she thinks. And she quickly looks away. Sips from the cup but tastes only bitterness. Feels unsafe. Feels threatened. I have to leave.

You're being silly, she admonishes herself. But a furtive glance tells her he is still observing her. Still strange. He has a sports bag. He could have anything in that. I better leave, she thinks. She pushes her chair back from the table. Collects her bags. Leaves her half-drunk coffee. Heads for the carpark. Checking back. Turning back to see if he is following her. The world is unsafe. Check again.

On the tram, a man gets off at the same stop as she does, waits to cross at the lights as she does. He carries a suitcase and there is something sticking out of it at one end. Something not tucked into the suitcase quite right. What's he doing with a suitcase anyway, on a tram and then on foot? How odd. Lights change. They cross. He walks behind her now, along the footpath on the right-hand side of the road. Both striding briskly. She in front, he following. Is he following? It doesn't feel right. It doesn't feel safe. She with her briefcase, he with his suitcase.

Her house is straight up this road for several blocks and then she will turn right into her street. It is too far to go with him behind her. She decides to take a small unnecessary detour. Cross the road. Stop and stoop to adjust her bag. That'll do it. He is in front of her now, and on the opposite side of the road. She has him in her sights. That's better, she thinks. That's being silly, she thinks. No, that's being smart, she decides. There is something odd about him. I don't feel right. I've taken precautions like this before. It's no big deal.

Later, as he walks far ahead of her, pounding up the hill with his suitcase, she crosses back, turns into her street. She suddenly feels rather sorry for this young, neatly dressed and handsome man, having to lug that suitcase such a long way. How much further must he go? Where is he going? Where has he come from? It is an ordinary, sunny afternoon in a leafy middle-class suburb.

In the supermarket line, her trolley half full. She nudges along in the checkout queue. Sudden awareness of her surrounds. Sudden awareness of her vulnerability. Anything could happen here. Someone could pull out a gun and start shooting. What's to stop them. Look at that guy. He could have anything up his jumper. It's not safe. I must get out. I better get out. She abandons the trolley, makes for the exit. She won't shop alone again for some weeks.

Midnight. Time to sleep. The TV stays on. The overhead light burns in full brightness. He is beside her, he will stay with her. She is safe. Still she cannot sleep. She can see past the bright light. She can hear past the TV. She is wide-eyed and wide-eared. She is on alert. The wind is no longer a soothing friend. It makes things swish and shake and bang. The cats are no longer comforting creatures. They make things swish and shake and bang. Is it an intruder? Is she safe?

Late at night, she hears an explosion from the street. And another. It is the sound of gunfire. Her body and mind are on red alert. The ghastly adrenalin rush moves her to action. She drags her sleeping children from their cosy beds. Assembles them all together in one room. She peers out the window. Trepidation. The world is not safe.

There is smoke, from a car. The backfiring of a car. The shame. The anger that it controls her so. That he controls her so.

We have police here this morning, the morning after, and we have three security guards here all day.

The parade of private security experts starts even today, the day after the shooting. Grey-suited men standing straight and tall, bespectacled, ex-police, polite, serious, knowledgeable. Lou and Greg tour the Clinic with them. Over several days and weeks, they advise about best options to upgrade security. Our new sophisticated security system—video surveillance, intercoms and locked doors everywhere—is up and running six weeks after the shooting. With it comes some sense of relief, but also a sense of sadness. The open and inviting ambience of our Clinic was assaulted, and now it will not be the same. There is far too much secrecy, taboo and fear we try to combat for our clientele. We hope that our new security does not echo back loudly all of the dark images surrounding women's fertility. Still, these days security measures like these are becoming more the norm in a number of businesses. So, we will have the Clinic as it was, and the Clinic as it is. The before and the after. But we are here just the same.

Ultimately these security efforts bolster staff sense of safety. But today, when nerves are frayed, and over reactivity of the physical and mental survival response is still at hyperalert, it is an extremely tough ask for Lou and Greg to be schooled in every possible security risk scenario facing our Clinic. This task will go on for weeks and it will take its toll.

The morning after, and through the day, I try to get around to every staff member. I ask questions and listen; I inform and listen. I listen and learn. Each day, for several days, will be a similar routine, same goals—normalising, reassuring, affirming safety measures, recognising staff's tremendous efforts, sharing the burden, I'm here if you need me, external consultants are there if you need them, here is up to date information, feel appreciated, minimise self-doubt. I aim to buoy their confidence in themselves, in their employer, in their workplace. My pride in our staff seems to grow each day. But each day there will be new questions, and new information, as the post trauma processing and process unfolds.

This morning, the mundane questions are basic but telling. How'd you sleep last night? Did you sleep like a log or hardly sleep at all? How did you go coming into work today? You know, someone just said they were driving in and thought they might just keep driving right on by. How'd you go? How did your husband/mother/kids react? How are they doing? And I'd listen. Listen and learn and try and make it okay. It's distressing, it's tough, but it's to be expected. Great effort you're here. Hang in there.

Some went home to supportive and sympathetic families, some did not. For some the phone lines were abuzz with the bolstering concern of other staff, friends and family. For some, there was silence or undermining criticism.

It is 6.00pm, Monday 16 July 2001. It is a date without any significance in her life—until now. Now it is forever etched in the calendar of her life. Her husband picks her up from the clinic. A smile. A hug. And then into the car. His steady reassuring presence. She can let go now.

Once home, she is embraced by her children's love. Their generous capacity to nurture is on display. The table is set, dinner served. Her teenage son has cooked up his speciality, tuna spaghetti. Her 10-year-old, in his karate outfit, has attended his karate class and home again thanks to her 19-year-old. They have done it all, for her. She is truly blessed.

The events of the day are splashed over the media. But the day's events wash right over her 10-year-old. Even when he sees it on the TV that night, he just observes matter-of-factly, 'That's where you work isn't it, Mum?' And he is gone. On to something else. Almost twelve months later when the court case brings it all back into the news, it is a different story. His mother is caught on camera for a split second and he sees it. Terrible connections are made and he doesn't like what they are. 'Don't go into work, Mum. I don't want you to go in there. It's not safe.'

But the events of the day are already more than media headlines for her older children. Her son was there when the call came in. He saw his mother frightened and agitated. He saw her disappear to a murder scene. Her daughter worked casually at the clinic. She filled in there just the week before the shooting. She worked at the reception desk, that very reception desk.

This is deeply personal. It is not just the news. Not just distant, shocking truths which barely touch. This is personal. So they must talk. She tells them about Inspector Rix's perspective. She logically states a case, 'I could shut myself up in a room and not go out into the world. But that's not living.' She offers what reassurance she can. Her husband supports her—and provides his own perspective too. They talk.

They know it is how it is. But still she feels for them. Unlike her, they do not think of death every day. For as long as she can remember, she thinks of death every day. It is the backdrop of night which allows the stars to shine bright. For half of her life she'd thought everyone thought of death every day too. After today, there will be more who think of death every day.

Some are not as lucky. Some go home to angry, fearful partners, parents, children.

I am being reasonable and firm, he thinks.

He is freaking out and being totally irrational, she thinks.

'You go into that workplace again and we're over,' he says, not quite sure what his stubborn fear has actually just said.

He can't handle that I might not be safe, she thinks.

It is a difficult, painful night. The threats and cajoling go on for some time. But eventually what lies beneath it all comes to the fore. And they are okay.

'I don't want to lose you,' he says. 'I love you.'

'I love you too,' she says.

They spend the evening on the couch looking through magazines. It is serious business. He points to this one, then that one, explaining this feature and that. She patiently looks and listens with wide-eyed amazement. Might this one suit best, or that? Can she see herself accessorised so, or so? It is a whole new world she has never really entered before. Perhaps it is funny, normal, or macabre. She cannot tell.

To sit with one's lover and shop for a handgun.

Almost cross that her family is so blasé about her coming in today, she sits in the staff lounge waiting for the kettle to boil and feeling a little neglected. She gets teary hearing how my family enveloped me in warmth and concern. She even feels a little envious of staff members whose families have been so anxious they have tried to stop them coming in today. Finally, 'I guess I'm really lucky. It's good they're not upset by it all. It's just… It would've been kind of nice if they'd worried about me a bit.'

Many staff become involved in harsh and unforgiving self-doubt. They ruminate on what they should have done, where they fell short. They are particularly judgmental and unkind to themselves. Eventually, over the next few days, they voice their considered opinions, their harsh judgments, their guilt, their attempts to find meaning and control where none exists.

'Next time, I swear, I'd just get out of here. Anything happens like that again, I'm out of here.' Janice, like others, critically and judgmentally, questions her actions of yesterday. She has a family depending on her, children. What was she thinking? 'I mean it. I'd just get out of here.' And she tosses her auburn tresses and sets her expression as seriously as she can. Then she is back to her job. Back to holding this place together. Back to keeping us going. Janice continues being a pillar of strength. She just keeps going. There's no way she is out of here.

Tracey is bold and wonderful in her recognition and sharing of her conflict at the time, 'I'm standing on the steps running up, then running down. I'm going up, the kids, think of the kids. You have to be alive for them'. Then running down again, 'Don't be silly. You're a professional. You should go and help.' Back up the stairs, 'The kids'. Down, 'Professional'. Up. Down. But she is still puzzled and unforgiving about this response. She is a gutsy person who has never backed off from protecting her own, even if it means a physical confrontation. She finds it difficult to accept her humanness, how much this troubles her. Not one to draw back, Tracey reassesses her life. She decides it is time for a positive change, decisive, major change. Two months later, Tracey resigns from the clinic. After ten years here, she tackles a different path, intends leaving the old one behind.

A fortunate few do not blame themselves, do not agonisingly replay their part in it all, but know that's how it is, how they are, how people are. For others, voicing their self-doubts, their guilt, their fears, is almost impossible. But through the next few days and weeks, they are voiced, if not to me, then to family, friends, or the consultant. Some cannot even recognise their conflict, let alone put it into words. It all happened too fast. It all is beyond comprehension. The feelings, or lack of feeling, is still a blur.

Ingrid struggles painfully with an unfair burden that she let Steve down. Her recriminations and guilt are merciless. She sees it over and over in her mind. Her rapid flight down the back stairs in 118. His wound. Her helplessness. Her rapid flight back up. She is a mother, a wife, a nurse, the first medically trained person at the scene. And she could not offer comfort. She could not help him. He needed medical skill far beyond hers. She knew it. She did what she had to.

Yet Ingrid erroneously and unfairly believes that what she did was not enough. The thoughts keep tapping at her mind. I should have been able to help Steve. I should have been able to comfort him.

It is devastating for her. It is unspeakable. And so she does not speak of it. For days, almost nobody knows the cause of Ingrid's despair. They do not know her fleeting, but emotionally charged role in this tragedy. They do not know her shock at seeing the man bleeding and dying, the man she could not recognise as being Steve. Her shock at her own helplessness. Her guilt at leaving him. The ruminative, torturing replay of it all. Her unfair but unwavering guilt and shame. Her attempts to commune with Steve's spirit and speak to him from her heart. Beautiful linking of the darkness of night and death, and the brightness of stars and the human soul. Steve's bright soul. Bid Steve farewell, come to terms with it all. The reason she cannot bring herself to come into work.

Kathy too is coming to grips with her helplessness to save Steve, her guilt at having failed him. She replays in her mind how she worked frantically on Steve's bloodied and lifeless body, pleading, 'Don't do this to me, Steven. Don't die.' But Kathy's guilt comes up against a healthy dose of medical realism too. She knows that she could do nothing for Steve. But still, she needs to know for sure she could do nothing to save him. She needs proof, evidence. A week after the shooting she finally asks, 'Any chance of seeing the Coroner's report?'

I make various enquiries. Every avenue I chase is the same answer. No chance, not for months, not until it is made public in court. And who knows when that will be? Finally, two weeks after the shooting, I ask Det Snr Sgnt Rovis. He is brutally clear and concise in his assessment that Steve was killed almost immediately.

'Can I quote you Lucio? A couple of staff need to know. They need something official that says they could do nothing to save Steve's life.'

Susan types it up. The content is powerful and unambiguous. As I read it I feel like I am violating some unwritten code of good conduct, like I am violating Steve's life. The truth is brutal. But the truth needs to be known. I wonder what impact it has on Susan as she types it. She types it meticulously, quickly.

The result is both pathetic and powerful. Five lines cantered on A4 paper, like some child's poem. I provide a copy to both Ingrid and Kathy.

> 'The fire power he had, even if Steve was
> shot in the arm he would have died from shock.
> That type of weapon has such high velocity—
> shatters bones. He had no chance whatsoever
> being shot in the chest.'
>
> Detective Senior Sergeant Lucio Rovis
> 31 July 2001

9

Yesterday This Day's Madness did Prepare
To-morrow's Silence, Triumph, or Despair
RUBAIYAT OF OMAR KHAYYAM

On my morning rounds to staff, I try to update them, keep them informed. This morning, Tuesday 17 July 2006, I tell staff that our external consultant will be here at 10:00 for an informal walk through. Her name is Deb Glowaski, and I'll be showing her round the place and introducing her.

I am pleased that less than twenty-four hours after Steve's death, we have a trauma psychologist arriving to be briefed and informally meet staff. On the basis of my talk with Simon, my intuition and my optimistic desperation, I am hopeful that she'll be right for us. If not, I'll go back to the drawing board.

The morning after Steve's death, Deb arrives punctually at 10:00am. Deb consolidates the reassurance and confidence which impressed me during my phone conversation with Simon. Deb's training and experience is extensive, and the combination of her past and current frameworks and teachers is particularly reassuring. Deb has trained and worked with Jeff Mitchell, but she is currently supervised by Ruth Wraith. Jeff is the fire fighter turned psychologist who developed a standard format for psychological debriefing of emergency service workers following disasters. From my own clinical training, I remember him as an extremely affable and engaging speaker who at that time was a welcome trail-blazer. Currently there is some controversy about critical incident stress management. In part this stems from its later uncritical and recipe-like use with victims of a trauma who are not emergency service personnel. There has been a growing recognition that not all people benefit from the 'talking about it' approach, and indeed a small number may be retraumatised by this process. I also have concerns around the apparent exclusion of the person's most important interpersonal attachments, that is, their families and partners. Critical incident stress management needs to embrace and harness the potentially health enhancing power of a person's family, rather than inadvertently catalyse its sabotaging potential.

In this climate, discovering that Deb is supervised by Ruth Wraith is a real plus. I worked with Ruth twenty years ago at the Royal Children's Hospital. Just weeks prior to the shooting, I read a chapter of hers, *Children and debriefing: theory, interventions and outcomes*, in a book published in 2000. The entire book is devoted to *Psychological debriefing: Theory, practice and evidence*, with chapters written by many of the leading lights in the field, and edited by Beverley Raphael and John Wilson, well regarded for their work in both grief and trauma. Ruth's chapter exudes the warmth and level-headed marrying of psychological theory with the realities of what it is to be a human being with our vulnerabilities and emotional attachments. Ruth showcases the sureness, flexibility, understanding and confidence in human recovery I value. She recognises the central importance of our relationships with the people we love and how these can buffer and protect if given the opportunity to do so. My first impressions of Deb are now comfortably confirmed.

Deb is a power dresser, down to earth, experienced, sympathetic, skilled, but with a likeable wackiness and sense of humour. Deb is young middle aged. She's seen more than her fair share of life. A variety of earrings in each ear suggests a healthy flouting of authority we are used to. Her modern, business-like dress and hairstyle mirror her other credentials. I am confident that our staff will find Deb familiar and approachable.

We talk for a while in my office. I provide her with a general background of the clinic and our work here. I brief her on a few themes which have already emerged from my discussion with staff, and through subsequent phone calls with her, tee up an all staff session for Thursday afternoon, requesting that Deb provide pertinent handouts for staff for themselves and to take home to their families. I'm a great believer in providing written information. It is something solid people can hold in their hands, take away with them, refer back to when they might be ready to take in, and consider, something they could not during the face-to-face session. It is something tangible and authoritative they can hand on to their family and friends to help explain what is going on. Family and friends then feel less helpless, more knowledgeable, and are more likely to offer the right kind of support.

Following our chat, I walk Deb around the clinic, telling her more about the place, our unique culture, introducing her to staff as we go. It seems the most natural thing in the world to be doing. This is the type of psychologist staff is used to having around, I think. Staff should feel at home with her.

And they do. It takes only a little encouragement from me for the small handful who recognise their need for an individual session to book to see Deb. We know that a more chronic course is more likely to eventuate when the trauma experienced is more severe, but also when other aspects of a person's life experience are present—childhood and adult histories of other traumas, pre-existing personality or mental disorders (usually stemming from the former, but also related to genetically determined and physical conditions) and poorer social and therapeutic support. I am relieved and pleased to hear the brief and positive feedback from staff members who clearly feel that their privacy and personal integrity is respected. It appears that Deb is able to find a good balance between recognising and validating the sometimes overwhelming nature of staff members' experience and feelings, and assisting them to tap into their own strengths, courage and natural healing processes. Her unique therapeutic style and skills seem geared toward short circuiting the likelihood of longer-term pathology developing from a normal human reaction to a life experience which is traumatically beyond the normal. Staff and I are happy with the timing and scope of intervention. It appears to have brought focus to understanding, healing and prevention.

Deb's initial arrival at the clinic includes the unpleasant initiation of being approached by the protesters. She is clearly puzzled and slightly unbalanced by them and deploys the same humorous bemusement we draw on in dealing with their fanatical intrusions. But the protesters are neither funny nor amusing. Their shenanigans, especially in the context of medical privacy and health rights, border precariously on definitions of stalking, harassment and threatening behaviour. We are not at all convinced that anti-choice personnel or rhetoric have not played a role in the tragedy which has befallen Steve's family and our clinic.

On the front page of *The Age* newspaper this morning, where the shooting is headline news, it is perhaps heartening at least to see both the group who stages protests outside our clinic, 'Members of Helpers of God's Precious Infants', and Right to Life, try to distance themselves from the gunman. Their choice of words is similar. The gunman was, 'not attached' to their group or their organisation. But the use of the words 'not attached' is not at all clear given the way both these anti-choice groups use it. Right to Life is reportedly 'not attached' to the US Right to Life, but 'the Australian anti-abortion movement did receive support and encouragement from the US.' As reported in *The Age*, a member of the protest group outside the clinic 'says the Melbourne group is independent from the US network, although Monsignor Reilly provides them with 'spiritual guidance'. Monsignor Reilly's spiritual guidance, on a web site emanating from his residence, The Monastery of the Precious Blood, calls on volunteers to flock to their local 'killing centres' to pray, and hopefully intervene before a woman completes the 'spiritual abortion' necessary before her physical one, and nothing makes up for your absence at the 'death scene'.

The Chairwoman of Right to Life in Australia, is further quoted, 'We would never condone this behaviour, but (the clinic) is a place of immense violence and it is little wonder that this has occurred. Some people will take the law into their own hands.' One of the protesters who struts his stuff outside our clinic, speaks in similar terms. For some reason at pains to point out that his group, the Helpers of God's Precious Infants, are in no way affiliated with high-profile anti-choice groups such as Right to Life, his comments rely on a similar logic. At least he made some touching comments about Steve. 'We are shocked and sad. We knew Steve reasonably well. He was a nice bloke and we did not wish him any ill. But we believe that violence begets violence. It's hardly surprising that abortion leads to acts of violence.'

Do their comments blame the victim and sympathise with the perpetrator? Do their comments try to justify the very violence and disregard for human life such organisations are vehemently against, while contending they are doing the very opposite? Is this rhetoric and doublespeak seductive and dangerous to the vulnerable and unwary?

The Victorian Premier, Steve Bracks, voices his disapproval of such comments and is reported in *The Age* on Wednesday 18 July 2001: 'I would have thought it would be a better time to actually keep quiet and to respect the fact that a security guard was killed rather than inflame the situation, rather than make comment and (gain) political capital out of it.'

In the aftermath of Steve's murder, we find it even more difficult than usual to tolerate anti-choice tactics. This includes routinely finding ourselves picking up the pieces of women who have unwittingly, and in a vulnerable state, accessed anti-choice 'counselling'.

Her dark hair hangs limp about a face washed out and sagging. She is mid-thirties, but under the weight of Life looks much older. She seems to contract into the clinic walls trying to be invisible and to disappear from all this. She looks neglected, alone and upset. Nicole is very early in her pregnancy and has travelled here from rural Victoria. Her partner is threatening to leave her if she continues the pregnancy and she already has children who need her care. She has a history of postnatal depression, suicidality and antidepressant treatment. Her partner, no doubt scared and scarred himself from the torture inflicted on those who are the loved ones of a soul dragged into the black abyss of serious depression, may be unable to provide the support she requires. He is noticeably absent.

This is Nicole's first visit to our clinic, but she is no novice to fertility problems. On the heels of postnatal depression, Nicole has undergone a succession of important fertility related events which see her now with an extensive history of reproductive loss. Within the space of two years Nicole has had a miscarriage, an abortion and sterilisation, a sterilisation reversal, and now this pregnancy. Undergoing a sterilisation at the same time as she had her abortion may have seemed expedient and sensible at the time. But it confounds two significant reproductive decisions and experiences, both with unique and intimate connections with Nicole's identity as a mother, a woman, a person. Combining an abortion with sterilization is rarely recommended. The sequelae for Nicole were difficult, and she ultimately underwent surgery to reverse the sterilisation.

Together with her distressed state these facts reveal a significant complexity and ambivalence suggestive of repeated reparation for pregnancy loss. Perhaps it harks back to her first miscarriage. Perhaps it reflects lost opportunities to joyfully mother her second child because of the catastrophic impact of her postnatal depression. Perhaps its roots go back much further to disruptions in her own attachment experiences as a child. It appears to be all three. In the realm of Nicole's fantasy, a pregnancy is romanticised, desperately wanted and easily incorporated into her day-to-day life. But the actuality of the pregnancy brings with it the realisation that she cannot cope with the additional pregnancy and parenting demands. She is vulnerable to relapsing into serious depression.

'I was psychotic you know,' she says matter-of-factly. 'Even though I've had some problems, you know, I've been doing O.K. I am not going back into that black hole ever again.'

The actuality of pregnancy brings with it a realistic and no doubt accurate assessment that the demands of another pregnancy and baby would overwhelm Nicole and place her and her family in serious jeopardy. So, her attempts to replace the loss are befuddled by the trying circumstances she is in, leading to an attempt to regain control which results in loss again, followed by an attempt to replace it. Again. And so it goes on. Nicole's situation now is no more conducive to continuing this pregnancy than when she was previously pregnant.

Understandably and realistically, Nicole also fears for her emotional wellbeing after the termination. As a clinician, so do I. No wonder Nicole is washed out and distressed. But of one thing Nicole remains steadfast. Nicole is adamant that she must terminate her pregnancy.

Articulating the links between loss and reparation, her own childhood of attachment disruption, insecurity and loss, an unwitting repetition in adulthood when faced with significant attachment milestones (such as becoming pregnant, giving birth, child off to school and so on) can at least provide self-understanding, a type of self-forgiveness and future insight. Nicole expresses the 'ah-ha' of insight as new connections resonate inside her. We discuss my contacting her doctor to ensure solid follow-up. Although the dangers to Nicole of continuing her pregnancy outweigh the dangers of terminating, I am very worried about her. I am happy to hear that she has a good relationship with her local doctor, sees a psychologist on and off, and could increase that contact.

Nicole proceeds to theatre uneventfully. No tears. Clear in her decision. When I catch up with Nicole in recovery following her abortion, she strikes me as relieved and surprisingly grounded and coherent. But it is very early days. Nicole's relief is a positive sign, but I know that she is likely to face a hard road ahead of her. She knows it, too. But for now, she impresses as strong, relieved and determined.

Eight days later, Nicole phones me. She spoke with her doctor, but her psychologist is away. She was clear that she made the right decision, but she needed to talk so she called an emergency abortion crisis number.

'I thought she was nice. She listened to me and I told her most of it. But she said I'd done the wrong thing. She made me feel worse. She talked about the baby being in pain and said that it will forgive me if I pray and I shouldn't have done what I've done. She said abortion is murder and women always regret it and they never recover. She said you should have never let me go through and the clinic is just a money-making business and if I phoned you, you wouldn't care. She told me my worst nightmare was going to happen. She said I should never have sex again and I should be tested for sexually transmitted diseases. And the way I was feeling I sort of believed what she was saying. She had me too scared to contact you, and she said I should look up their website instead. I went for two days and I couldn't eat and I couldn't sleep. I got shirty with the kids and I knew I had to do something. So finally I called your number. And I spoke to June. And I just wanted you to tell June, Thanks. I know I made the right decision', she sobs. 'I know I had to do it. My kids come first. I've got to be there for my kids.'

And I bolster and validate Nicole's common sense, her love for her family, her courage and her strength.

'False providers' was the term used in the September 1995 National Health and Medical Research Council (NHRMC*) Draft paper—Services for the Termination of Pregnancy in Australia: A Review* to describe 'services which aim to dissuade women from using abortion services but which are advertised as providing abortion counselling and support. Women who contact such services when seeking to terminate a pregnancy report problems of delay, false information and unprofessional approaches to both information giving and counselling.' (p. 16). Anti-choice pregnancy/abortion 'counselling' services are listed in the 24-Hour Emergency section of telephone directories, and elsewhere. An unwitting public assumes that these emergency numbers provide a service by qualified professionals linked to a government or accredited organization, but instead the 'service' is no such thing and has an ulterior, but not readily apparent, anti-choice agenda—once conceived, a pregnancy must be continued to term. A woman contacts such services with the expectation that she is the service's client, that her welfare will be their primary concern, and that the service will make appropriate referrals according to her needs. But the true clients of such organisations are pregnancies, not women.

Perhaps Steve's shocking murder has galvanised something inside us. Perhaps we are hanging our heads out the window and yelling, 'We've had enough and we won't take it anymore.' But how to change things so that ordinary women are not verbally abused accessing a health clinic, so that women will not suffer unnecessary emotional and physical pain when all they are doing is trying to lead responsible, caring and valuable lives. Women and men have a right to medical service and a right to privacy without unwanted intrusions into their physical and emotional space. We live in a democracy and people have the right to protest, but that does not mean they have the right to protest wherever, whenever, and however they like.

Positive political interest in our circumstances continues into the next week, but in a personal, face-to-face way. I arrive at work the following Monday, just one week after Steve's death, to see listed in my appointment book for 12:30, Natasha Stott Despoja. Although politicians have graced our clinic in the past as patients, Senator Stott Despoja, leader of the Australian Democrats, has contacted us and asked to meet with us in the wake of the shooting. Lou asks me to greet and look after the senator.

Senator Stott Despoja is an impressive young woman. Beautifully dressed in neat skirt suit and delicate shoes, she exudes a warm but business-like charm, and she bowls me over with her keen and genuine interest in our situation. She poses sensible and insightful questions, listens attentively, and follows up with more perceptive and highly pertinent questions. She spends an hour with us and I try my best to ensure that she is introduced to every member of staff as I show her through the clinic. Staff members are chuffed by her presence and interest, and discussion with all of our doctors impresses as stimulating and informative. The senator uses her visit to become fully briefed on our clinic.

Senator Stott Despoja's visit is widely reported in the media. Her article in the *Herald Sun* two days later features a photo of her speaking with a security guard at the gate of our clinic, and is headlined, 'We must speak out about abortion.' The article is a class act, just like the senator. It concisely but incontrovertibly speaks up for women's access to abortion, speaks against the continuing intimidation by anti-choice protesters by providing a 'bubble' or 'buffer' zone within which protesters cannot enter—this would mean that the protesters must stand no closer than, say fifty metres to the clinic entrance. In her beautifully thought out, calm and reasonable way, Natasha points out, 'If women wish to take up the offer of 'counselling' from the protesters, I am sure they would take those few extra steps, especially when many have had to come from interstate.' There is nothing militant here. It all makes absolute sense. It is based on basic respect for women's self-determination and integrity.

Sadly, I realise that it is utterly out of character with the way Australian leaders of political parties usually behave around the issue of abortion. Usually, politicians side-step it at all costs. Tip-toe around it quietly as if it is a sleeping dragon. When I sat on the Board of Family Planning Victoria, we seemed to be in constant anxiety that the government would make a trade-off with politicians holding anti-choice views—the elimination of the Medicare abortion rebate if they concede on another matter. It can be a dangerous flaw in our democratic system that a tiny minority can at times hold the balance of power. At that time too, RU486 was in the lime-light. RU 486 is a pill providing a safe, non-surgical means of terminating very early pregnancies. It has been used in Europe for years, but it has not been allowed in Australia. As I recall, at that time an uneasy alliance of the anti-choice religious right and hard-line feminists, paradoxically joined to ensure that Australian women could not have access to RU486. The governing Liberal party happily made a deal to forgo RU486 in return for the anti-choice independent Senator Brian Harridine voting with them on privatising Telstra. Is this the way we want our politicians making decisions about women's reproductive health? Disgraceful.

The majority of Australians believe in a woman's right to access abortion services and believe in a woman making such a decision within the confines of the doctor-patient relationship. This belief is also held by people who themselves would never countenance having an abortion, no matter how shocking their situation, but who also maintain a basic respect for women and their capacity to make responsible and moral decisions for themselves. They can see the dangers in judging, controlling and imposing their beliefs on others whose situation they cannot fully understand.

She is thirty-six and given birth to two children. The eldest is the child from her first marriage. That child shares the white Anglo features of her parents. Some years following the tragic death of her husband, she finds love again. This time with a Pakistani man whose time here as a student led him into a successful business and Australian citizenship. Her second child closely resembles her father, the child's appearance dominated by her Pakistani ancestry, including striking deep brown eyes with exquisite long eyelashes. It is only natural that people are curious. How can these children be siblings? How can she be the mother of the child with Pakistani features. Is the child adopted? How can her husband be the father of her first child? At times this woman becomes impatient with the repetitive and insensitive looks and comments from others. But what is most disturbing, are the racist taunts directed openly towards her, her husband and her children.

Now she is pregnant again. But it is not a joyful occasion. The circumstances of her pregnancy are shocking. While on holiday overseas, she was raped. She is pregnant because of the rape.

Now she is trying to cope with the trauma of the rape, a pregnancy resulting from that rape, the care of two children, and a family situation of loss and new hope, far more complex than most, where she and her children daily reckon with racial ignorance and hostility.

Even people who hold deeply to their belief that life begins from the moment of conception and that this life should take precedence over the life of the pregnant woman, can struggle to maintain this view when the pregnancy is the result of rape. Rape is often the exception to their rule. There would be almost no one who would judge this woman harshly if she decided to abort this pregnancy.

But the impression which grows throughout our session together is that although she now presents to our clinic because she is pregnant to a violent stranger, in itself this fact might not provide an exception to her beliefs about pregnancy and abortion. Her anti-abortion religious affiliation and views are strong. Somehow, her overwhelming concern for the pregnancy seems to make the rape recede into the background. Her awareness that the pregnancy is part of her fights with the knowledge that it is also part of the rapist. She is acutely aware of many of the difficulties she may face. But her focus on the baby she might bring into the world seems to give her courage and strength. I am amazed by her fortitude and spiritual strength. I hope that she and her family will cope with the difficult decision she makes.

She goes away to continue her pregnancy. If all proceeds well, in thirty-two weeks' time she will give birth to a baby sharing the genetic make-up of herself and of the indigenous African man who raped her.

No woman wants to find herself in the situation where the only, the least worst option is to have an abortion, and no woman wants to be bullied about it. Natasha Stott Despoja is a woman who stands up to those who bully. And it is wonderful. Her response perfectly captures the current situation and we feel a validation and recognition which is sustaining. I send her a letter of thanks on behalf of staff. At the Federal election later in the year, Natasha gets my vote.

Another who takes on bullies is Labor Senator Chris Schacht from South Australia. A day after our visit from the Australian Democrats' leader, I am pondering that the next day I might sleep in a little and not get in quite as early as usual. The idea is growing on me. In fact it is feeling absolutely necessary and luxurious at the same time. Then Lou tells me that Senator Schacht will be arriving at the clinic at 8:00am and can I make sure I'm there to greet him. Apparently Senator Schacht intends standing out the front holding his own placard declaring women's right to abortion and engaging the protesters in his own unique way. I can see this senator has a somewhat different style to Senator Stott Despoja.

Although I arrive early, I somehow miss the Senator's demonstration. When he re-emerges in the clinic for my guided tour and introductions to staff, he is like a mischievous kid who's taken on the cruel schoolmaster. Apparently he stood there and gave them better than he got, heckling, arguing and holding his placard aloft. And when I see him I almost feel sorry for the protesters. He is huge, about 6'5" and full of energy.

We ask him to sign his placard for us, which he graciously does. Then lengthy discussion ensues which travels far and wide from the central issue of abortion, engages numerous different staff and is fascinating and exhausting. While other staff join in for short bursts and then disappear to their work, I am the constant. The energy of the man is way beyond mine at this stage of the game. But his presence is strongly appreciated. His idiosyncratic antics particularly so. We are saddened when Senator Schacht loses his seat at the Federal election later in the year. We need more politicians who are prepared to stand up for women's reproductive health rights.

Although we still do not know the gunman's motives or associates, if any, the assault on our clinic catalyses other political groups in the days and weeks to come. The Socialist Alliance and the Pro-Choice Coalition hold a demonstration at Parliament House in Melbourne on Wednesday 18th July, deploring Right to Life rhetoric and urging the legislators to take abortion off the Criminal Code—the only medical procedure in the Crimes Act rather than the Health Act. I've sometimes pondered if it were men who conceived and bore children, would their access to abortion face such institutionalised stigma and their privacy and rights to seek medical and family planning treatment be questioned and placed in jeopardy? I am reminded of a confronting Family Planning poster years ago depicting a heavily pregnant man.

There is a dinner held in honour of Steve in Sydney some time in July, and on Wednesday 29 August there is a public meeting in Sydney titled, 'How will we defend abortion rights?' sponsored by Women's Abortion Action Campaign. Their leaflet raises the concern that legislation to restrict anti-choice picketing outside abortion providing clinics may lead to 'similar legislation targeted against trade union and other progressive groups.' I don't think so. We are talking about a very specific situation—women's health clinics. North American and Canadian examples demonstrate that bubble legislation enforcing no go zones for picketers around health care facilities can provide a simple and easily enforced solution which recognises fundamental rights 'of privacy', 'access to medical counselling and treatment' and 'the right to be let alone'.

Meanwhile we all keep going. Following the lead of Janice, June and so many others, most staff work even harder at being here. They are here more often, plugging the holes left by those who cannot be here. I will work full-time until the end of July, and then slowly draw back. But others will take on more in an ongoing way to ensure the Clinic can meet its obligations to our clientele.

Liz is one of these. On that day, the day Steve was killed, Liz helped Kate move patients from the lounge back to recovery. Liz is a red-head, new millennium, nursing version of Mary Poppins. Spit spot manner, bright eyed optimism and full of energy. Liz forgoes her study so she can take on the role of charge nurse. It is a huge sacrifice, but Liz embarks on it all with cheerful and conscientious zeal. Her positive disposition is contagious, and the nursing staff bounces back with gusto. Liz's bright outlook also spreads to other staff outside the theatre complex. I am a grateful recipient of her warm optimism on many occasions, as she moves with warmth and efficiency amongst her staff and her patients. It is so difficult to reconcile the caring which pervades this place with rhetoric of murderous and depraved action.

June sits opposite a patient who holds fundamentalist anti-choice beliefs and carries them into action. She has in fact protested outside our clinic. Yet she is here requesting an abortion.

June offers her compassion and nonjudgmental assistance. She raises the possible conflict for her: given her strong beliefs, had she looked at all possible ways of being able to continue her pregnancy?

Well it is all disgusting and so on and so forth, and she of course is nothing like anybody else we see here, of course her circumstances are so much worse than anybody else's and she has no other choice and she will deal with it, thank you very much. Her claim to the moral high ground within a psyche where compartments of thought, emotion and action are apparently sealed off from one another, ensures she proceeds through theatre uneventfully, intent on continuing her life as if nothing had happened.

As a counsellor in the clinic room, June hopes that this woman can carry it through. As a counsellor outside the clinic room, we also hope that this woman might allow her own experience to soften her stance towards other women taking a similar path—terminating a usually unplanned and highly problematic pregnancy.

It is not unusual for women to think that they believe one thing about abortion only to discover that they actually believe, or have to do, something quite different. In the abstract, one view. When it's personal, it's different. In the deeply personal situation of being unintentionally pregnant, thoughts and feelings can take a U-turn. How many times have I heard, 'Well I've always been pro-choice and thought if I was in this situation I would have an abortion, but I'm not sure that I can have an abortion.' Or conversely, 'I've always been against abortion, I never thought I'd ever have one, but I really think I have to have a termination.'

So we know what we're doing here. We know that women and their families need our support, validation, respect, knowledge and medical care. But do the protesters have any idea what they are doing? Do they know what they are involved in? Who they are connected with? How they impact on others? How many would keep going if they knew? Do they really know what they are doing?

His unruly hair peeps out from a well-worn beanie. His beard is unkempt. His nostrils are oblivious to his own body stench. No one takes more than a fleeting glance at him. Such is the way with the general public and the homeless. Avert your eyes, avoid the guilt, the riff-raff of society are invisible.

It suits him. He can appear and vanish like a phantom. He has cycled and walked for days. He knows his plan. Just one or two little things to sort out. But he has intelligence, cool cunning, and moral outrage on his side. He knows what to do. He knows how to stop them.

Now he stands with them—they who understand. They who helped clarify his thinking, seal his resolve, and bolstered his intent. They who stand with him. Their words ring true. They share his recognition of evil. They deplore the killings and they demand their revenge. Violence begets violence. Murderers deserve to be murdered. The precious little ones need to be protected. They get that. They get that we should force people to abandon their ideas of aborting the children. He's seen the literature. He knows the score—the score on babies murdered and murdering doctors terminated.

Yet, what amateurs they are. This mob doesn't have the guts to carry through their beliefs to their logical conclusion. They can't take it the next obvious step. And yet it's that simple. He worked that out pretty quick smart. Yeah, they have the right idea. And while he feels an almost unbearable discomfort standing so closely amongst others, the others he has grown to loathe and avoid, these others at least share some like-minded values. Indeed he almost feels some comfort standing here with people who know what the real evil in our world is. It is a rare feeling to touch him, a feeling from long ago, like an apparition rising from a lake in the early morning mist. A touch both warm and chilling.

He finds himself physically shaking it off. It is a distraction. He is with them, yes, but he is better than all of them. He knows how to put their words into action. He knows how to do it.

When he first made contact with them, he was unsure. December 2000 it was, six months ago now. Before his trip to Sydney in March when he held up a placard of a foetus, outside Radio 2UE. A lot of good that did. And what was he thinking telling the police his real name, then. Just a small slip up. He'd got his act together really well since then. He'd stolen the Winchister rifle and ammo from that Park's store that dark night in May. At least he'd left the store owner a nice note saying he'd be back to pay—with interest, 'Sorry Mate, I had to do it.' And he'd made up a special bag for the rifle, cut and fastened it so he could use the rifle while inside the bag. Had to revamp the rifle a bit, but not a problem for someone like him. Just glued two half washers alongside the hammer so the hammer wouldn't be obstructed by the bag when he fired it. How clever is he. Then he'd made the 800-kilometre journey from his forest humpy to set up camp a few kilometres from the clinic in Templestowe's Candlebark Park. It was only then that he'd realised the totality of the work God had in mind for him.

Anyway, soon after he stood with them for the first time, he met their head honcho. Yep, it was just this past January. Rather disappointing then she was, not a leader at all. She sent him away to put his proposal in writing. She has the right ideas: violence breeds violence; murderers should be murdered; an eye for an eye; abortionists should all be shut down—no matter how. He'd given her the opportunity of discussing things with him face to face. Gone to her office—twice. Eyeballed her. Talked to her. Taken her his manifesto. The meetings had not turned out as he had anticipated. Just as well he'd been smart enough to use an alias this time—signed his letter to her as Peter Sweeney. Ha. Just in case—you never know who you can really trust. Wasn't gonna have all his great plans messed up by some bureaucratic cow. But on reflection he understood why. She has her role and he has his. It all comes down to him. And he is up to the task.

No one else can see it all with the clarity he has. No one else can make it right. He's done his homework. He's doing it right now. Ha. And no one even knows. His plans are moving along well. The method he will use is developing, coming alive in his brain. Practicalities he is overcoming, working through. No one knows he's here. They'd be hard pressed to identify him—been on his own for so long. No photos of him like he is now—made sure of that. No one knows he's here. But he knows Them. Oh he knows Them very well. Know thine enemy. And he does. So well. And they don't even know it.

He's got his makeshift campsite tucked away nice and deep in Templestowe. A nice little campsite, a sheet of plastic over some rope tied between trees. Ah. His home away from home. A nice little spot to make his plans, gather supplies, do his reconnaissance. And he is brilliantly, meticulously methodical as always. Makes lists of items he needs. Painstakingly, ingeniously, crafts gags and torches from scavenged twigs, filthy old rags and grubby foam bound together with twine. Engineers superb door-handle locks using wires, nuts and pieces of metal tube. Prepares containers of

Kerosene. The wonder and power of his own hand—his gloved hands, his free mind. Brilliantly planned. It will be brilliantly executed. There will be no escape for the slaughterhouse and its murderers. They will perish in the fire of the Almighty. The eternal fires of Hell await them. And he sees everything that he has made and behold it was good.

But now he stands with the good people. Well, better than most. Right ideas, but just can't take it that final step. Guess that makes 'em hypocrites like the rest of 'em. But he can't help having a soft spot for them. After all, it is as if they have helped him clarify his travel plans, pack his bags, wished him a happy journey. At least they are trying. They have some idea. Just no guts.

Won't they celebrate when it's done. Won't the overseas web pages go to town about it. What a score. And no one will even know. No one will ever link it to him. He can go on then. Go on with God's work. Save more of the innocent.

He knows that the killings are continuing only metres from where he stands. But it is only a fleeting discomfort. Instead he relishes the fact that he knows what the future holds for these baby murderers. And he knows the role he is to play.

So, it's good cover standing here with them. They're not too nosy. Happy to have him with them. Bless you, they say. Oh, you've come to help the precious babies. Thank you, they say. Here to do Jesus' work. They hand out their leaflets, show their awful photos, try their sidewalk counselling. While he blends in. Draws no attention to himself. Carries out his surveillance of the death chamber.

He stood with them once before, and he might do so again. He is the one who knows how to put a stop to it and he is the one with the guts to pull it off. It's just a matter of time—maybe three weeks, maybe six. It's just a matter of time.

So, he stands on the pavement at the front of the Fertility Control Clinic. He stands shoulder to shoulder with the protesters. For now, he is one of them. And he is welcomed and encouraged by them.

10

What we call the beginning is often the end
And to make an end is to make a beginning
T. S. ELIOT

So although we have no idea what the protesters are doing here, we know what we're doing here. It is tough keeping going. Maintaining as much routine as possible is mandated by our commitment to our patients, but also is recommended by best critical incident stress management practice. Routine is ultimately helpful to the majority of staff. We are under no illusions that it is best for everybody. We know that it is asking a lot of staff and that eventually staff will need respite, need to take leave to recuperate. But for most, now is the time to be together and to continue on. With a couple of exceptions, there is a sense of sharing and belonging which is uplifting to staff. Although there is ambivalence and fatigue too, most want to be in here with their colleagues. They gain sustenance and support from this special bond.

I have the easier job of it. Not just because I was not in here when it happened, or because I am not suffering the adrenalin surges and the fear, but because most of my time is spent on matters related to the 'critical incident'. When I have to involve myself in my usual clinic job of caring for distressed or bewildered patients, rather than our staff, I feel a little off balance. I must shut out all the trauma—the before, the after, what needs to be done. And I find such mental compartmentalising difficult, but necessary.

He sits close, but no comforting arm around her. Words and feelings are not his forte. He is a problem-solving man who works using his strong body and calloused hands. The counsellor who saw his wife initially has spoken with me about her, worried by this woman's distress and predicament. So I know this woman's pregnancy is the result of failed, but conscientious, contraception. I know she feels their situation is dire—two young children, one labourer's salary, burgeoning demands from previous partners and children. Like her partner she fears they cannot cope financially or emotionally with another child. Her children will suffer, their relationship will suffer, he might not be able to cope. But I also know she is only here to please her partner. She does not want to terminate the pregnancy. She has said that she could not live with herself if she aborted her pregnancy.

Today nothing has changed. It is tough going for her partner, as it always is in this type of situation. Once a woman is pregnant, although a male partner may have input to the pregnancy decision—offer support, raise concerns, make threats, break off the relationship—ultimately he has no control over the final decision. The only time he has a real say is prior to conception. If he does not want children now, he can take on conscientious responsibility for contraception or have a vasectomy or discuss all this with his partner prior to beginning a sexual relationship or… And things can still go wrong or change. Once pregnant a woman may feel very differently than when she was not pregnant. Couples present to us anywhere on the continuum from long-term stable relationship to early and unstable, or no ongoing relationship. She might make a decision inextricably binding him to her, to a child who is biologically theirs. He will face legal, financial, moral and parenting decisions and responsibilities he may feel he is unable to face. But he has no real say now—once she is pregnant.

Sometimes it is the other way round—she is clear that she could not cope if she continued the pregnancy and is comfortable about terminating the pregnancy, while he is desperate for her to continue. Again, he has no real control over the outcome. but he will suffer the repercussions.

With this married couple today, we discuss the difficult life he has led and leads. Of course he sees abortion as an easy solution to this problem, but with clear assessment of his partner's risks if she terminates, he quickly appreciates that she cannot do it. She has come into the clinic to try to terminate this unplanned pregnancy because of her love for him, but because of her love for him and life together, this pregnancy is precious to her, she cannot have an abortion.

He wants her to be okay, but he feels painted into a corner. With the new reality he faces now, he tries to engage with my encouragement to problem solve. We brainstorm strategies to assist him, how to help him cope with another child if the pregnancy proceeds and all goes well. I do not mean to minimise the plight of this woman—she will certainly face a substantial load. But his support and confidence will be crucial to her capacity to cope, and while she may be vulnerable to serious emotional problems if she were to terminate her pregnancy, he is vulnerable with its continuation.

They leave to continue the pregnancy. He books a consultation to discuss vasectomy.

For some staff the familiarity and order of their work is a relief and provides a sense of normality and control they might otherwise find elusive. Others find it exhausting, and a couple ultimately leave their employ at the Fertility Control Clinic.

Early in the afternoon on 17 July, Leslie sits on the fire escape steps crying frustrated, angry tears.

'It's disgusting that we are open today.'The day after what happened on the 16th of July.'

Together, we look out over the gloomy panorama of our small rear car park, brick walls in every direction, a muddling sky above.

'I can't go home but I don't want to be here.'

She is deeply troubled. Tears continue to spill from her eyes, emotions spilling from a mouth now sitting awkwardly in her sad, angry face. She is a gutsy, determined woman who came into her workplace today under considerable aggravation. Like some other staff, in the immediate wake of the shooting, Leslie's significant relationships have been seriously destabilised. An experienced and dedicated member of our staff over several years, Leslie is one who yesterday bravely re-entered recovery to care for patients, not yet knowing what was happening, risking her own safety. Although yesterday's events confront staff with a range of emotions, the intensity of Leslie's distress concerns me.

Leslie's words about disgust are not what I expect to hear, not from Leslie. 'Disgust' is a word typifying the stigma of abortion we all rally against. It doesn't make sense. But 'disgust' is a word I hear from another nurse. It is an interesting choice of word, I think. Not 'unfair' or 'unhealthy' or 'disrespectful' to Steve—though I would have thought the opposite would have been true, that is, disgusting and disrespectful if we closed the clinic when Steve's job was to ensure the clinic's service remains safely accessible. Unlike Leslie, this other nurse, young, assertive and career-minded, started here recently. She apparently was quick to contact the nurses' union in the wake of Steve's death. Perhaps she thought they would offer assistance. Perhaps she thought it her responsibility. This nurse was not in here at the time of the shooting. Perhaps it was her way of looking out for her colleagues. Perhaps she is reassessing her abortion views considering her work here, her own recent happy pregnancy, and now, a murder at her workplace. A murder at your workplace can certainly trigger a reassessment.

Abortion is a challenging issue, and she is one of a new breed of nurse, young, educated with career commitment and ambitions, apparently modern feminism in action, but who has not made the connection between her own freedom to choose and pursue her goals, and the freedom to control her fertility. Fertility out of control can be devastating. And we do not have the 100% reliable, comfortable, affordable, safe contraception, and we human beings are definitely not 100% reliable and rational. We are passionate, forgetful, shy and ignorant. Add to that women's vulnerability to sexual and physical abuse, and abortion must be available, accessible, affordable and acceptable.

Anyway, the Australian Nurses' Federation (ANF) has apparently responded to her call very promptly. When I sit with Leslie on the steps behind the clinic, the ANF have just phoned and spoken to Leslie. Did their phone call trigger Leslie's demoralised and angry outburst? I am fairly clear that it did a few hours later when the ANF representative contacts me. If her phone call to Leslie was anything like her phone call to me, the odds are stacked towards her contact being highly detrimental. Little more than twenty-four hours after our workplace homicide, and I am reasonably sure that the ANF offered Leslie no sympathy, no reassurance and no assistance, just insensitive interrogation and interference driven by a misplaced sense of self-importance. Apparently the ANF has yet to develop a practical and sensitive policy and protocol about its contact with a trauma-affected workplace—one that considers the appropriate style, content and timing of contact and the training needs of ANF staff carrying out this important responsibility.

The phone call from the ANF may be the last straw for Leslie whose situation is already complex, and deeply and unfairly conflictual. Now, she feels she can't go home, and she can't stay. She has to go home, and she has to stay. Leslie is a fighter. But the enemy is difficult to identify. She is in danger of being a victim of friendly fire. I ask Lou to tell her to go home. Go home Leslie, look after yourself. It won't suit everyone to be in here today. We want you to look after yourself.

Leslie gathers herself together. She stubbornly and bravely stays and works the next two days as well. Her staff need her. Her patients need her. But on the Friday, Leslie takes the leave she had planned to take before all this. She knows she will not return.

There were twenty staff members in the Clinic at the time. Another twenty-six patients and their relatives and friends. The theatre complex cushioned the majority of patients from the impact of yesterday. And the morning tea time slot and clinic rear exits would have ensured that if the gunman's real intentions had come to fruition, many would have escaped. But there is no doubt that without the actions of our heroes, many would have died. The potential devastation is too much to imagine.

That leaves another ten staff who were not there on the day. A couple of these came in as soon as they heard the news and took part in the staff session three hours after the incident. They speak of feeling compelled to do so. Other staff fought the impulse to drop everything and come in. Some were unsure of whether their presence would be helpful or whether they might get in the way. Others were unsure whether they really wanted to be here anyway. There is no set protocol for such things. Others, because of their responsibilities, could not have come in even if they had wanted to.

Marion was not in the clinic yesterday. Today, she is working in the admissions office, and she is unusually despondent, quiet. Even after yesterday's events, Marion's demeanour seems unusual for her. Marion is modern, late forties, with short neat blonde hair, and a slender build. With clients, whether counselling or administratively, Marion's whole manner is one of gentle sincerity and reassurance. There is a softness in her voice, a motherly aspect to her attentiveness. With staff, she can occasionally shock the socks off you, conspiratorial and gleeful whispers. No one can dislike Marion.

'How're you doing?' I ask. There is a blankness in her features which I have never seen before. It almost does not look like Marion. Where has she gone?

'Well, I just don't think I can say anything. I mean I wasn't here. So if I say anything it'll just be, "Well how can she know anything, she doesn't know, she wasn't here".'

I smile outwardly with warmth and affection for Marion. I smile inwardly with relief. This we can deal with.

'Marion. It's great that you and I weren't here. That's a good thing. We can do things that other people can't. You and I can do things other people can't. But, we have also been affected by this. We are also part of this.'

On Thursday when we have our formal staff session with the external consultants, Lou figures that Marion can operate switch while it's on.

'No, she definitely has to be there,' I say. 'It is crucial that Marion is there.'

Lou soon understands and agrees. So much we don't know, so much to learn. Another business generously lends us a receptionist. Marion is part of the session, just as she is part of it all. The Thursday session with our external consultants is attended by twenty-eight of our thirty staff members.

Some days later, and staff are still understandably desperate to thank our heroes more substantially and do something for Steve's families. Yet the physical and emotional energies of staff are ebbing. Not so Marion. Marion takes it on board and comes up a wonderful idea and sees it through. With her daughter helping, Marion shops for beautiful paper, sorts out a delicate and stylish computer font, and sets it out in simple elegance. It is important for our recipients that we do this quickly and Marion completes it all in a time frame I would have thought impossible. She nags and organises and chases so that every staff member has taken it home and returned it. The first page is presented almost like a certificate. To our heroes, it says:

The families of the staff at F.C.C. want to thank you for your valiant effort on July 16th, 2001.

They feel you have saved the lives of their loved ones.

They also feel that, but for your efforts, they may have lost the people they love.
Thank you.

To Steve's family, it reads:

The families of the staff at F.C.C. want to show their appreciation to Steve. They feel the sacrifice of his life saved many lives and that he must be held up as a hero.
We want you to know how grateful we all are.
Thank you.

On several attached pages, contained within tasteful borders, are the deeply personal handwritten messages of thanks from all staff members and from their family members—sons, daughters, fathers, mothers, partners, husbands, wives. Some are in the shaky hand of the elderly. Others are in the awkward hand of children. The rest are in the fluent hand of writers whose age is somewhere in between. As I read what they have written and as I write mine, I have to watch that my teardrops do not stain this work of the heart.

Marion's thank you's are sent out less than a month after the shooting. The feedback from all of our recipients is wonderful. Marion's idea is therapeutic and healing for all of us, and for them. Our heroes and Steve's family shed tears when they read it. They tell us they bring it out to read when they feel down. It is inspirational. Our heroes' shattering involvement and Steve's tragic death gain some positive meaning and purpose in the eyes of those who matter most.

You can do things that other people can't, Marion.

While staff generally keep going now, several have days when they just cannot come in.

'Kate isn't here. She hasn't phoned. It's not like Kate.'

'What?' says Janice, emerging from a counselling session. 'Still not heard. That's not like Kate.'

Kate does not show up to work on Thursday, three days after the shooting. No call. Nothing. Her phone is constantly engaged. We've been phoning every so often throughout the morning. We are all becoming a little worried. Yesterday was a tough day for Kate. It ended in tears, angry, weary, feeling unappreciated tears. We know that's to be expected. We know that she's probably just decided to curl up and shut out the world for a while. Of course that's what she's doing. Still, it's not like Kate, even in the circumstances.

June and I decide we'll go to Kate's house at lunchtime. It is the whole staff get together today with Deb and another of the external consultants and I am meant to meet with them at 1:30pm, prior to the formal staff debrief at 2:00pm. We might make it back in time. Time slipping away.

June being June, knows the way to Kate's house. Me being me, does not. June being June, drives. Me being me, feels relieved not to have to drive.

It is a pleasant Victorian house surrounded by garden in inner suburban Melbourne. We knock on the front door, with its pretty stain glass window. 'She's probably just, you know, didn't want to come in today,' reassures June as we wait. But we both aren't sure. It's been a week of being unsure about so many things.

Kate opens the door with a weary smile. Dressing gown, slippers, dishevelled blonde hair. A surprised but welcoming, 'Hi.' A warm, 'Come in.' Relief. Kate just couldn't speak to anyone today. Just could not get out, needed a day to slop around, stay incommunicado at home, hide away.

We have gone to Kate's to check on her, to offer support if she needs it. But it is typical of the whole crazy situation this week that it is Kate who gets us a cuppa and makes us a couple of cheese sandwiches. Forgetting to eat has been very easy this week. The busyness and lack of appetite see to that. But nourishment is crucial and Kate's cuppa and sandwiches are just the ticket. We sit and we chat and we laugh.

But there is no way Kate is leaving the house today. She will miss the debrief, but that's okay. This is what she needs - time out, time to herself. One of the major items to be covered in the debrief is to reveal the contents of the shooter's bag, the arsenal of ammunition and flammable material. His motivations may not be known, but his intentions are now crystal clear. Kate knows about the bag already. Stay home Kate, slop around. Thanks for the cuppa and sandwich. Look after yourself, see you when we see you, but don't stay away too long.

Kate returns the next day.

June battles on, respite from her nausea coinciding with various healing opportunities. After our very first staff get together on the day, June is free of the nausea briefly. Following the formal debriefing on Thursday, June's nausea leaves her for several hours. Steve's funeral provides solace from her body's bilious state for more than a day. Over the ensuing weeks, after many entrances and exits, June's nausea finally seems to take its final bow, like a reluctant aging actor recognising that its time is finally up. But while on leave in November, and driving through the countryside, the nausea makes a dramatic, unexpected, and fortunately brief, reappearance. June has just passed the turnoff to the Killanbutta State Forest.

Gradually over the next five months, everyone will suffer some form of physical ill-health and will take sick leave and well-earned recuperative leave. A couple of staff will be hit by more serious illness. Some will be baffled by the weirdness of the symptoms which assail them when it appears that we are back to normal.

'What the heck do you reckon these are, Susie? I've got these great itching welts all over me.' says Janice in early December. 'Is it the detergent I'm using? Some sort of bite? Something I ate?' And she embarks on serious detective work, sifting through the ingredients of food and chemicals and routines which make up her daily grind.

Somehow Janice has weathered the traumatic storm. Despite torrential emotional downpours and cyclones, she proves herself to be a most accomplished trauma sailor. Though being flung up against odds which at times she feels she cannot overcome, Janice will not, and does not, give up. I marvel at her stamina, sensitivity and humour. By the end of July, Janice has dealt with one hundred and one urgent tasks, large and small. She sorts rosters where staff are in short supply, slots herself into any gaps. She arranges nourishing sandwiches for meetings, ensures that absent staff receive their pay amidst various uncertainties, employs new staff either via personal contacts or advertisements, makes herself available to troubled staff and Steve's troubled family… The list goes on and on. And so does Janice. She just keeps going.

But come December, following closely on the heels of a miserable cold and aching teeth requiring dental treatment, Janice endures a very uncomfortable few days, beset by these most unwelcome and ugly welts.

I am reminded of the many clients who have consulted me over the years, where their physical illness seems to be a concrete bodily expression of the numerous sayings we use every day to describe the various predicaments of the human condition. The woman who consulted me with trichotillomania, that is, recurrent pulling out of her own hair to the point of noticeable hair loss. We worked out together that she was indeed literally, 'tearing her hair out with frustration'. And with this our understanding and therapy strategy fell into place. The numerous seriously physically ill teachers who found their way to my rooms in the mid to late eighties following the interpersonal calamities wreaked by the agony of ruthless school closures, mergers, cutbacks to student welfare, assault of teachers by students or vice versa. It was almost invariably the most hardworking teachers who were presenting, their bodies finally convincing them that they had to take a break. They variously were sick of confronting 'a pain in the neck', 'left speechless', or like our staff in the immediate and subsequent aftermath of Steve's murder, felt 'sick to their stomach', 'couldn't stomach what had happened', or had 'lost their taste for life (food)'.

At the same time, in my work I have often become angered with the way physical illnesses and symptoms, especially those of women, have been dismissed as all in the mind, hysterical, neurotic and so on. Endometriosis was one such distressing condition which tarnished and pained women so, before it was recognised as a medical condition requiring medical treatment. I am horrified by those extolling the view that our physical illnesses are somehow brought on by our psychological selves and we can prevent or cure them if we would only think the right way. This sort of thinking and sermonising can be exceedingly unhelpful and outright dangerous. We are a physical being too and as such are at the mercy of the infinite bioentities which can corrupt our systems.

The body-mind interaction is wondrously complex and little understood. I see no contradiction between my latter views and the former. And I see no contradiction in viewing our staff ill health, including Janice's itching welts, as tangled up with the previous five months of trauma and challenges.

With the help of antihistamines, Janice's welts gradually subside in one area, only to erupt somewhere else. Finally, after several days, they go. Something perhaps has 'got under your skin, Janice?' And why not? The word 'inflammation' seems especially apt in the context of Janice's previous five months. Inflammation is 'the reaction of living tissue to injury or infection' and it is closely aligned to the word 'inflame—to arouse or become aroused to violent emotion… To set or be set on fire.'

Janice's body, like the rest of her, tells it like it is.

Or perhaps Janice just ate something funny.

11

Do I dare
Disturb the universe?
In a minute there is time
For decisions and revisions which a minute will reverse
T. S. ELIOT

It should be her who got shot, not him. If only she had been in yesterday, perhaps it might have been her, not that nice security guard. He didn't deserve to die. She should've died instead—all still, at peace. Except she'd probably go to Hell. Definitely will after today. And tears well up in her eyes. She doesn't have the courage to kill herself anyway. She couldn't do it to her four beautiful children.

Her hair falls out in clumps. It is limp blonde, greying and balding, so thin in parts she can no longer hide her hair loss. It's been even worse since she found out she was pregnant. No one knows she is here today. Not her husband, not her children, she has no friends. No one must know what she does today. No one must know how she will cancel the life inside her. The shame, the guilt, the sin.

Louise's first visit some days ago was not as unpleasant as she had expected. In fact she couldn't remember a time when others had been so gentle and concerned about her. Louise even felt almost nice about herself in there. But she lives a lie and she knows it. A wife and mother amongst the struggling lower middle-class, surviving on one wage so their children have a mother at home. She couldn't do anything else anyway, she doesn't have any skills, and he won't let her. She's not even good at being a mother and wife. It was only right that he threw the dinner onto the floor last night. Of course the rice was overcooked, she had been preoccupied with today's appointment. She never asks for anything for herself, it is always for them. And it is for them that she will do this.

Yet a part of her knows that it is for herself too. If she is really truthful, she absolutely does not want to be pregnant, to go through it all again, at her age too. Why God did you do this to me? She didn't dare tell him. Would he have made her have the baby or would he have made her get rid of it? She does not know and does not want to know. This way is best. She is at least determined to do this on her own. And what do those people out the front know? Why did they have to rub her nose in it? Of course she had walked straight past them, pretended she was not entering the clinic then went around to the staff entrance. But they are right of course. She deserves to be insulted and chastised. She is a murderer—well, soon will be. She has given life to four. She failed to give life to one other, when she so longed for a baby—its new smell and soft skin. But she had lost it. Her body expelled it, something wrong so deep inside her that it had to escape. And now, when she does not want to be, she is pregnant. When she cannot bear it, she is asked to bear it. Now, she will end it herself, and she will pray to God that He will keep her children safe. She dreads that He might take one of her children away, but surely He already did that, all those long years ago. And she feels a fleeting but sharp pain in her chest. Oh, God, send me to Hell if You must, but don't hurt my children. And Louise wishes she had been here yesterday.

Louise is a 'prior to theatre'. She presents today, 17 July, for her previously arranged theatre booking to have an abortion of her seven-week pregnancy. Like roughly half of our patients facing a problem pregnancy, Louise first presented some days earlier for her consultation. Then, if she decides to terminate her pregnancy, theatre occurs on a subsequent day. That way, women have a chance to feel more comfortable with everything, usually feel more confident about their decision, are more aware of what to expect before and after their operation and have had a chance to discuss future contraceptive issues in a meaningful way, unfettered by anxiety about a new environment or surgery. Or, having faced the real option of an abortion, decide to continue their pregnancy. This contrasts with 'Today' patients who choose to have their consultations and theatre all on the one day because of work, childcare, geographic or other reasons. Even so, if after her initial counselling consultation, a 'Today' patient impresses as unclear about her decision to terminate, she will be encouraged to think further or consult me before rebooking.

Louise is one of the many who keep their appointments today despite the well-publicised drama of yesterday. She is one of the many women who rely on us continuing to function today. But unlike the majority of women, Louise's presentation is cause for concern. At her initial consultation, Vicki was so worried about Louise, she offered her the opportunity to speak with me, but Louise declined. Vicki wisely ear marked her card for counselling again prior to theatre. June speaks with Louise briefly, but in the absence of any improvement on her initial presentation, June refers Louise to me. On her patient card, following the greater detail of Vicki's initial entry and June's briefer one this morning, I summarise our encounter thus:

17/7/01. Louise presents as clinically depressed. She reports never having reached out for psychiatric or other assistance. She has not told anyone, including her husband re pregy.

I have referred her to Doveton CHC, but I am not optimistic that she will contact them, although she has said that she will. Forbade me from contacting her local doctor. Would provide no details of GP. Says no prior self harm/suicide altho has thought of it. Sig hair loss. Clear re decn but feels she is a bad person.

It is not often I see a woman whose self-esteem is so battered. Louise sees no hope that she can be helped out of her depression and sees no reason why she should be assisted anyway. She feels she does not deserve help. She feels her situation is hopeless. She feels helpless, bereft of self-worth, well-practised in serious self-downing, passivity and isolation. Given all this, Louise's attendance at our Clinic and her decision to terminate her pregnancy in fact signals the presence of some positive energy, self-concern and direction. Although there is clearly much that she is unable to speak about, she has at least shared some of her feelings and experience. She has at least been greeted with kindness, understanding and validation of her as a worthy and respectable person. All we can do is hope that her contact with us is a positive one so that she might be more likely to reach out for help in the future.

More than an hour later, I catch up with Louise in recovery. She is grateful and relieved, but still unwilling for me to contact her doctor. I invite her to contact me at any time. When she leaves us, she is alone. The literature we gave her earlier is probably all disposed of. But her secret is safe. I never hear from Louise again.

The day following the shooting death of our security guard, the day following the cordoning of our clinic as a crime scene, we have no idea how many patients will attend. We have no idea how many will cancel. Some have to arrive today or their health would be put in jeopardy. Already it appears most patients attend for their appointments. It is surprising, and yet, perhaps another indication that reproductive crises wait for nothing. Another indication of society's error in trivialising and stigmatising these urgent, stressful events in women's lives. Events which we all too often forget impact on men's and children's lives too. I wonder if we will be inundated with calls from patients who were here yesterday and need assistance related to what happened. But we are not.

So, although I wonder what the protesters think they are doing here today, the day after our security guard was shot dead in cold blood, we know why we are here.

It is 10:30am. Barely twenty-four hours after Steve's death. I walk Deb, our consultant trauma psychologist, around the clinic, introducing her to staff as we go. I have already caught up with many staff prior to Deb's arrival. I am able to brief her on particular areas of concern, as well as more general information she needs in order to understand us, our clinic, our work, and the impact of yesterday. As we walk through the room where women wait just prior to moving on to the change rooms and then to theatre, a woman is softly sobbing here. She looks to be in her forties, well dressed and groomed, but still she looks neglected and so alone.

'Excuse me, Deb,' I say, and approach this woman who is clearly upset. I sit down beside her. We chat very briefly. She was in here yesterday. When it all happened. It does not take much for her to accept my suggestion that she move to another area to wait a few minutes, so we can talk in more detail.

'Is she upset about the shooting?' asks Deb. One might expect so. But in the scheme of this woman's life, the shooting is the last thing on her mind.

As is often the case, women initially tell so much of their story, but withhold some. The line between telling and withholding often appears arbitrary. A woman says in front of her boyfriend that she has had one previous abortion. Later, on her own with the counsellor, she says that she has in fact had two, but didn't want him knowing that. One was somehow acceptable, but two was not. And then, what is important to say and what is not? So, for a variety of reasons, it is not uncommon for women to reveal to me more of their circumstances than was first known. Audrey is no exception. Yesterday, through embarrassment, fear and determination, Audrey did not give a full account of her reproductive history. Audrey has had four miscarriages. She and her partner endured three years of IVF before finally, painfully, accepting that they were not going to be one of the lucky few successful IVF participants. Three years on a roller coaster ride where early pregnancy diagnosis took them to the peak of hope, and the dreaded, cursed appearance of blood swept them to the lows. In the end neither she nor her partner dared hope at all. And yet it would always be there, hovering behind the dread. They had invested so much. Could they afford to give up on it? Could they afford to keep going? IVF came at great cost, physically, emotionally, financially.

They slowly divested themselves of anything linking them to having a child. They learnt to invest their energies in other directions, other activities. But the damage was done. Their relationship ended and the loss multiplied. The child they craved was forever a fantasy—their child who looked like him and her, and who would be named Jack or Kate. The flawed medical gods had not known the cause of the couple's infertility, who was to blame. He was driven to prove his potency, now living with a woman ten years younger. The loss, the pain.

And now, three years later, she is pregnant. She had stifled her initial excitement and feelings of being so special. She could conceive naturally after all. After everything—she was pregnant.

Then the gloom had descended. How ridiculous, after everything. Too old, no partner, too late. Could she do it on her own? What would people say? Single motherhood. How could she cope? If she went on, could she go through another miscarriage? It would miscarry anyway, and if it didn't, what if it was abnormal? The tests, the medical monitoring, the finances. She'd be the oldest mother in history. She might die before it was twenty. Has three years made so much difference? And it has.

She has adjusted to childlessness and has adjusted to single life. She is perhaps happy with her childless but busy life. Yesterday she was clear, but now that clarity is all in the past. Now, on the threshold, her yearnings overwhelm her, and she is lost. She wants to scream at the Gods, the unfairness of it all.

Documented risk factors for post abortion emotional problems do not include IVF participation. That may be because much of the research was carried out pre-IVF, or just didn't think to investigate IVF, or the number of women in samples was just too small, or... There is only so far the abortion research can take you. Like all research the answers depend on what questions are asked. Clinically, a woman with a history of IVF, especially unsuccessful IVF, sets off alarm bells when she is presenting for an abortion. If she has got this far, it is never simple. She needs time to think and talk and be encouraged to reflect on the resources she might bring to motherhood now. Know that the decision she makes is one which is true to herself, one which she can live with.

No wonder the shooting doesn't matter one iota.

So, we know why we are here today, we know we are needed and we know the paths we have travelled to bring us here. But what of the shooter? Is he a disgruntled partner? Has he accompanied a woman here in the past? Is he disgruntled because we respected his partner's decision to have an abortion, or disgruntled because we respected his partner's decision to continue her pregnancy. And if disgruntled, how did he move from disgruntled to homicidal. Is he connected to international or local anti-choice groups? Is he working alone? Do his actions have nothing to do with our work here? Did he just select us on a whim? Does he have a vendetta against doctors? Nurses? Day procedure centres?

And we know nothing.

His mind has energy to burn and his ideas amaze him. His intellect and daring is extraordinary. They just keep coming, he can barely keep up with them. He leans back against the trunk of a tree, pen poised. Get it out and get it down. The Truth. But let's have a bit of fun with it too. Don't make it too easy. He must challenge himself, keep himself fresh, and demonstrate how smart he is and how awfully stupid they are.

The smirk on his face disappears as concentrates. He loses himself in it. It is all consuming and he is meticulous. By the time he has finished, it is another masterpiece of wit and Truth. Whether they'll ever be able to crack the code is one thing. Whether they'll ever understand it if they do, is another. And he laughs uproariously. Laughs to the heavens. How bloody awful They are, the lot of'em.

On the paper is an array of apparently meaningless letters cut out from a newspaper. It is the alphabet at its most frightening. Letters painstakingly selected, cut and glued to relieve the boredom and drive of an obsessed mind. In his head, the message is pure and clear:

Anyone who protects sewerage is sewerage and will get treated like sewerage and the same goes for anyone who works for or with or who patronised sewerage. By the time I get through there will not be an abortionist in Melbourne left deathless. We will now see if the Vic Police are in the same class as the Nazi Gestapo and try to protect these slaughters.

12

The Moving Finger writes; and, having writ,
Moves on; nor all thy Piety nor Wit
Shall lure it back to cancel half a Line,
Nor all thy Tears wash out a Word of it.
RUBAIYAT OF OMAR KHAYYAM

Somewhere between 3am and 4am, my mind becomes a whirl. I don't fight it, I get up and I write. The aching pressure to say what needs to be said, to write it down, in letters to our heroes.

I leave the warmth of the bed willingly, with relief, to gather my dressing gown around me, walk across the cool vinyl of the kitchen floor, and allow my thoughts to tumble out. It is Wednesday, less than forty-eight hours since Steve's death. It is my first foray into early morning writing, and I feel compelled to hand write the lot and ask Susan to type them up. Susan and I are a team when it comes to correspondence. I frequently have to reply to doctors who have referred women to us and whose difficult circumstances mean they end up seeing me. I don't have ready access to a computer at work, and so I handwrite and Susan types. She turns my almost illegible scrawl into dainty, professional letters. No matter that it is her rostered day off. No matter that I could do them all on the computer, copy onto a floppy and so on. No, Susan has to type them up. Besides, Susan is losing sleep worrying about our heroes. Susan, like us all, is needing to say, Thank you, and so much more. It will be therapeutic for Susan to type up a thank you letter, I rationalise. This will be our initial, brief letter. The least intrusive way to thank them. Marion's more personal and more satisfying thank you still lies dormant in her imagination.

And so, I handwrite, and first thing I have to do when I get into work is phone Susan up and ask her to please come in. And if she can't? I get teary just anticipating this—I realise I am sleep deprived and irrational. I rationalise that the tears I know will pour from me at work today will be good permission giving for others. Not that they really need it.

It is quiet and peaceful at this early hour. I open wide the vertical blinds of the kitchen. It is pitch black at first, then the darkness takes on some familiar shapes as the day moves towards dawn. The shifting movement of a tree here, the solid edge of the neighbour's fence there, a glow of luminescent plant life, all held within a deep blue hue. I fill the kettle, flick its switch, rinse the coffee plunger. Soon I am sitting at the kitchen table, a pile of scrap A4 paper to hand, an empty mug, the coffee biding its time, 'til finally the coffee pours fresh and steaming, its energising aroma filling the room.

I don't know how my words come together to make sense, but they do. I might be sleep deprived and feeling vulnerable and unbalanced, but my words are how I want them to be, and how our staff want them to be. In my scrawl, illegible to almost all but Susan, I write a short letter for our three heroes, to Tim, Sandro and Brett.

The Management and Staff of the Fertility Control Clinic wish to convey to you our sincere and overwhelming thanks for your efforts in ensuring the safety of our staff and patients on Monday morning.

We appreciate that your actions were carried out at great cost to your own personal wellbeing. We also understand, much to our regret, that this may impose a special type of burden on you and your family.

We would like to take this opportunity to invite you to contact our Clinical Psychologist, Dr. Susie Allanson, if at any stage you think we may be able to provide you or your family with assistance or information. Unfortunately media coverage can misrepresent actual events and cause confusion and distress.

We understand that you already have information about the Victims' Advisory Unit.

Our heartfelt thanks again for your courage.

My comment about the media is aimed particularly at Brett, although I cannot know what impact media reports have had on the others. Brett had been sitting on the other side of the waiting room-reception door, opposite Tim, when Steve was shot. One minute, in bored, waiting mode. The next, hyper-alert, grabbing the shooter's weapon and running like the wind, sprinting through the clinic and down Wellington Parade, Winchester rifle in hand. Some fifty meters along, detouring into the florist shop, directing the florist to phone Emergency Services, placing the gun behind the counter—out of harm's way at last. I worry that Brett might not realise that we know of, and appreciate, his courage.

I write letters to Steve's mother, Shirley, and to Steve's partner, Sue.

We wish to express our deepest, heartfelt sympathy to you and your family. Steve's tragic death has devastated all of us here, all the more so because Steve died in his role of protector of the clinic, our staff and our patients.

Steve was a relative newcomer to the Clinic, but he already had impressed staff, patients and people in the neighbourhood with his warmth, outgoing friendliness, intelligence and calm manner. Steve impressed us all as a person of high quality who had a genuine interest and concern for people and life. Over the years we have had several security guards and Steve definitely had something special. His unique presence had eased the distress of numerous women, men and children having to run the gauntlet of the right to life protesters. Steve went out of his way to make himself known to staff, and staff in turn looked forward to their chats with Steve each day about everything from the weather to atheism. We all felt reassured and bolstered by him. We were all saddened by the recent death of his father and impressed by the quiet, selfless way he approached this loss.

In response to Steve's death, Clinic neighbours and patients have left flowers at the Clinic, often just with an accompanying card 'these are for Steve—he was a really nice bloke.'

Please accept our deepest sympathy and please do not hesitate to contact us if we can be of any assistance to you or your family.

Later that day, June writes her own thoughts and we include this beautiful note with my letters to Shirly and Sue, saying that June, as our Senior Counsellor and a celebrant, would be happy for her words to be used at Steve's funeral.

As a celebrant, I have often used the following words in funerals— 'Death follows life as sure as night follows day—it is the natural order of things', but it is not the natural order of things to be gunned down by a total stranger in your place of work in the prime of life. And we, as a society, need be very angry about this and other random acts of violence. We need to work on building a society where people have a respect for individuals and their freedoms.

We didn't know Steve for very long, but everyone who met him liked his friendly manner. I have a friend who walked her baby granddaughter past the Clinic each day and she said how nice he was and how he spoke to her and the baby every day. Other neighbours in the area commented on his friendliness.

I always thought it was a hard job standing out in the cold for hours and would take him a cup of tea if I had a spare moment. I had taken him a cup of tea that morning and he was always very appreciative. My chats with him were usually short ones but when he told us that his father was dying I had some long conversations with him about how he was feeling, the importance of the funeral and the importance of his participation in the funeral. He obviously loved his family and the grief that his mother must feel now after just losing her husband is unspeakable.

For the rest of his family, his mother, Shirley, his partner Sue and his children we can only say that our hearts go out to you and you can be proud to be part of the life of this gentle, caring man.

We are grieving and trying to cope with the horror of what happened but it cannot compare to the loss that all his family are experiencing. We can only hope that each day you gain the strength to carry on.

As the clutter in my head finds a comforting coherence on paper, slim fingers of light stretch out from the early morning darkness. It is still quiet inside, except for the echo of words which demand to be written. The kettle steams, the aroma of coffee revives me again, back to the kitchen table. I begin another letter, this time to the media. Tears and anger. My scrawl becomes worse.

We wish to thank the many individuals and organizations who have expressed support after the shooting death of our security guard, Steve Rogers. To all those who have offered support by e-mailing, phoning, sending flowers and cards or speaking out in the public arena, we thank you.

Steve had been with us for the past two months, but in that time he impressed staff, patients and our neighbours with his friendly, warm, intelligent and calm approach and concern for others. Many of the flowers left at the clinic have been accompanied by the simple words, 'These are for Steve – he was a really nice bloke.' We are devastated by Steve's death, and we express our sincere and deepest sympathy to Steve's family.

We cannot overstate our gratitude and debt to the three men whose quick and selfless actions ensured the safety of the staff and patients in the aftermath of Steve being shot. In the context of this traumatic event, their valiant actions may unfortunately impose a special burden on these men and their families.

On the day of Steve's death, a structure and process for psychological debriefing and ongoing therapeutic support was instigated by clinical psychologists within and external to the clinic. We offer our unconditional support to our staff and other individuals involved. We ask that the media respect the privacy of individuals struggling to come to terms with this tragedy.

We thank the police for their conscientious and sensitive handling of this case and support them in their endeavours to get to the truth of this shocking violation.

We find abhorrent the failure of Right to Life to condemn this violent act. We are appalled by Right to Life's insensitivity to Steve's family and to our staff and patients. In attempting to use this tragedy to perpetuate their own fanatical agenda, they have not only condoned this unprecedented violence, but also appear intent on inciting other individuals to violence.

We wish to reassure our patients, colleagues in the health profession and the general public that the Fertility Control Clinic will continue to provide the highest standards of care. As our protector and friend, Steve will not be forgotten, and our efforts to maintain the health service he died protecting will be our enduring mark of respect to Steve and his family.

This, our only public response, is printed as a Letter to the Editor in *The Age* on the morning of Steve's funeral. It is the lead letter and is headed, 'Thanks to nearly all in shooting tragedy.' There is a photo of Steve in uniform published alongside. I am pleased. Despite their grief, I hope his family is too. We arrange for the letter to be published in their local newspaper as well.

On Lou's insightful suggestion, I write a letter to Steve Bracks, Premier of Victoria

The Right Honorable Mr. Steve Bracks
Premier of Victoria
Department of Premier and Cabinet

Dear Mr. Bracks,

We wish to express our gratitude for your words of support during this tragic time. You have bolstered our staff and patients during a time filled with doubt, fear and devastation.

We would like to take this opportunity to seek your understanding and assistance in our ongoing concerns with Right to Life's intimidation and harassment of patients, staff and passersby on a daily basis at our clinic.

The behaviour of so called 'protesters' at the entrance to our clinic each day clearly oversteps the behaviour of peaceful protest. They display obscene and offensive material, such as large coloured photos of dismembered fetuses. They intimidate and harass anybody passing by or entering the clinic—staff, patients, neighbours and the general public. They position themselves in such a way as to physically encroach on people's personal space and at times chase women and their families as they try to enter our clinic by an alternative entrance. Staff and patients are daily called 'murderers' and it is not unusual for these demonstrators to follow women and their children from our client's car to the clinic all the while abusing them verbally. There have been instances of children as young as four years old being told by an anti-choice fanatic that, for example, 'your mother is going to kill you baby brother or sister.' One of our security guards resigned from her job last year after face to face death threats from one of the demonstrators. The long list of such disgraceful behaviour seems endless.

The Clinic has spent tens of thousands of dollars seeking legal advice about how to remedy the situation so that our staff, clientele and the general public can pass by or enter our premises without such harassment. We have sought advice from police and local council, all to no avail. Even in the wake of the tragedy, police were apparently helpless to move anti-choice protestors away. The right to peaceful protest appears to be sanctioned and protected above all else. Our view is that this behaviour does not constitute peaceful protest, but is harassment, intimidation and a threatening physical encroachment on people's access to their work place and access to a health service.

Our staff includes a gynaecologist, other medical practitioners, theatre and general nursing staff, a team of pathology scientists, a counselling team, and reception and administrative staff. We provide a full range of family planning services including termination of pregnancy, vasectomy and contraception, as well as other important women's health services (pap smears, colposcopies etc). Women and their families present to our counselling team with a range of issues and our gynaecologist and clinical psychologist also run their private practices at the clinic.

We provide a crucial and vital health service to the people of metropolitan and regional Victoria and other states (notably Tasmania). In the wake of this tragedy, we respectfully ask that you consider our concerns and do all in your power, whether through legislative or policy initiatives, to allow our staff and patients to go about their business in a safe environment and unfettered by threats and harassment.

So on Wednesday, two days after Steve's death, the writing done, and the morning well and truly awake with light, I set out for a walk and then into work. I am not suffering any of the distressing fear and jolting hyper alertness of other staff. I have not experienced shock of an extreme adrenalin surge, or the terror of running from, or running towards, an unknown assailant who has shot a work colleague. I am just me, running on empty and feeling emotionally vulnerable. As soon as I approach switch this morning, my bag filled with my early morning scribblings and my lists of things to do, I am a sobbing mess. Kate gently comforts me, 'Susie you're doing so well. You've done so much.' Six hours later our roles are reversed. Kate angrily tearful and me trying to comfort her.

And that's the way it is. That's the way we are. Despite their own distress, staff rally for others, and others rally for them. And it is not just in the immediate aftermath, it continues for weeks, months.

She enters Joan's office to ask a routine question, she thinks. And she is surprised. Surprised by how close to the surface it all still is, unexpectedly drawn out and soothed by that special something in Joan's sensitive and knowing gentleness, Joan's simple and perceptive comment. Unexpected tears spill and words expel in a cracked, staccato voice. And Joan is there with her sensible strength and warmth, a sturdy shoulder to cry on. Joan shares the burden, and when it is Joan's turn, Marion is there. And when it is Marion's turn, June is there. And so it goes. We pull together and draw on each other's strength. Now and for a long time to come.

So, this Wednesday, less than forty-eight hours after Steve's murder, I have a good cry and then phone Susan. Her youthful cheery voice carries across the line, 'I'm just back from gym. I'll jump in the shower and I'll be in. Of course I don't mind. I'll be in there soon.' And she is.

Susan collects all my scrawled pages and a wad of clinic stationery. She hides herself away in one of the unused consulting rooms with the typewriter, sits tall and graceful and pounds those keys. She types and types and types. Until now, I do not realise just how much I have written in the frenzy of my mind and the quiet of the morning. I feel even more guilty now, but also more thankful that she is here. Susan good-naturedly rebuffs my guilty apologies. Of course she is happy to come in, she wants to help.

And the letters are done, ready to get the nod or small changes from Janice or the directors. Susan has transformed my terrible scrawl into immaculate, professional letters. We are a team, she and I.

Over the next three days I am surprisingly productive in the wee small hours. Letters, letters and more letters, and updates for staff are written before dawn, but not by hand. I never do that to Susan again. Ever after I use the computer - type, save on a floppy, take it into work.

Friday early morning, I feel compelled to write what I call 'a silly little something' to give out to staff. So, I don't fight it, I type it.

IF YOU HAVE:

Listened to someone's story

Shared your own story

Let others see your emotions—whatever they are

Kept your true feelings contained and hidden

Given a hug or a sympathetic ear to a friend and colleague

Provided yummy sandwiches and cuppas for comfort and sustenance

Phoned someone to check how they're going

Phoned someone to share how you're going

Avoided the phone and avoided talking

Felt the most distressing feelings and reactions in your life and kept going anyway

Felt very little and kept going anyway

Felt pretty good about how you're going and kept going anyway

Felt the most distressing feelings, thoughts and reactions in your life and took time out

Felt you've lost control over what goes on in your head and how you behave

Leaned a little heavier on your usual crutches and even tried some new ones

Felt like chucking it all in, but you're still here

Looked at your world as if it's totally foreign and unkind

Felt unappreciated and undervalued and misunderstood

YOU MUST BE ONE OF US!

HANG IN THERE—WE LOVES YA!

PS. Monday may or may not be particularly difficult given the nature of anniversary reactions. Give ahoy. We are here for you.

I look at it feeling a little embarrassed and think staff might think me totally crazy. Too bad, I have to write it. That day and the next, staff feedback is surprisingly positive.

Finally I clack away on a draft letter to the Chief Commissioner of Police, Christine Nixon. Like the letter to Premier Steve Bracks, this is in response to Lou's request. During everything, Lou has the wherewithal to see the bigger picture. It has all gone too far and we are hanging out the window yelling, 'We're not going to take it anymore.' This letter requires a bit of discussion and fine-tuning and is finally sent a week later.

Christine Nixon
Chief Commissioner of Police

Dear Chief Commissioner,

We respectfully ask your assistance in ensuring the ongoing safety and wellbeing of our staff and patients in the wake of the recent shooting death of our security guard, Steve Rogers.

We have appreciated the sensitive and professional manner of the police team led by Detective Senior Sergeant Lucio Rovis and Chief Inspector Rix. Our concerns are with the chronic situation where the right to protest by Right to Life/anti-choice groups has taken precedence over the rights of individuals to safely access their place of work, safely access a health service or safely pass by our clinic. We believe that in our post trauma predicament, anti-choice groups' continuing threatening presence is intolerable and is not consistent with the Victoria police force fulfilling their duty of care to us and to the people of Victoria.

The anti-choice groups which daily assail our clinic, patients and passersby are not engaged in peaceful protest or a peaceful demonstration. Rather they are engaged in harassment, intimidation, threatening behaviour, abusive language, and the display and dissemination of offensive, obscene and graphic material. The latter includes, for example, poster-size and pamphlet pictures of dismembered fetuses, and fabrications and misinformation threatening disastrous consequences for women having an abortion. The former includes unreasonable and intimidating encroachment on people's personal space all the while abusing them verbally. For example, it is quite the norm for these anti-choice 'protesters' to chase clientele for some distance as they attempt to enter our premises at the main entrance or by an alternative entrance. Or they walk closely beside or behind staff, patients or the general public while calling them 'murderers' and couching their fanatical rhetoric in a quite personalised way, 'you're wearing red today—the colour of the blood of the little babies you kill'. They have also targeted children as young as four in this way, 'Your mummy is going to kill your baby brother or sister…'

Amongst health professionals it is well recognised that such tactics can be psychologically and physically harmful, especially when targeting people already feeling vulnerable and in a high state of anxiety associated with the stressors of facing an unplanned pregnancy, operation, abnormal pap smear or other health-related medical or counselling consultation. Our clinic provides a range of family planning and women's health services and our Gynaecologist and Clinical Psychologists run their private practice from the Clinic.

The concerns noted above raise serious questions about the Victorian police duty of care to Fertility

Control Clinic patients, staff and the general public of Victoria. The recent homicide here adds another dimension in considering the dangerousness associated with anti-choice groups placing themselves directly outside our Clinic. At this point in time, the motives of the gunman are not known. We do not know if he worked alone or if he has accomplices. In a climate where Right to Life appears to have condoned this violence and where anti-choice groups' behaviour outside our clinic has not abated one iota in the wake of this tragedy, we are understandably fearful of a copycat attack, or even worse. As you are aware, the gunman was well prepared to completely massacre the entire staff and set the Clinic alight. We have lived with the behaviour of anti-choice groups on our doorstep for years, and an untold number of adults and children have endured significant harm because of it. In our post trauma predicament, we are now overwhelmingly concerned that their continuing presence is intolerable and is not consistent with the Victoria police force fulfilling their duty of care to us and to the people of Victoria.

We respectfully request your assistance in this matter and await your reply on this urgent matter.

On Monday, one week after Steve's death, I hand out three short schedules for staff to fill in if they wish. Each is about how they have been over the past week, since the shooting. They can hand them back to me if they wish. The schedules are to promote staff awareness of the normality of certain symptoms and awareness of improvement. It might also alert me to somebody who might be needing extra assistance.

The first is called the Positive and Negative Affect Schedule (PANAS). It lists a range of positive and negative emotions and the respondent circles to what extent they have felt like this on a scale from 1, not at all to 5, extremely. It is interesting to observe that amid the expected 4's and 5's next to 'scared', 'angry', guilty' and other distressing emotions, many staff also indicate strong feelings of pride, determination and strength.

The second is the classic trauma schedule, the Impact of Event Scale (IES), which lists a number of sentences reflecting the common avoidance and intrusive distress experienced by people following a traumatic event. Respondents rate how often each statement has been true for them over the past week. Statements like, 'I think about it when I don't mean to', 'I feel as if it hasn't happened or isn't real', 'I try not to talk about it', 'Pictures about it pop into my mind', 'Other things keep making me think about it'.

The third is a home-grown schedule which lists basic functions—eating, sleeping, exercise, drug intake, work attendance and so on, known to be commonly disrupted following a critical incident. To this I also add 'Family support' and 'Worry about a family member.' Respondents check whether these have been the same, less or more than usual.

Staff also receive update memos such as the one I pass out eight days after Steve's death:

> If you are having any concerns about your natural recovery versus the need to see a psychologist for an individual session, please do not hesitate to contact either of the two psychologists we met last Thursday.

> Deb will be popping in tomorrow late morning. We will probably have another whole staff meeting with Deb and her colleague within the next month.
>
> Do not hesitate to discuss any concerns with me.
>
> Hope the basics of eating, sleeping etc are improving. EXERCISE of any type can make a really positive impact.

All of this information is included in the staff folders we organise on Wednesday, just two days after Steve's murder. The folders are to combat any sense of alienation, being taken for granted, or feeling left out of the information loop. I want all staff to be able to see all relevant information and the supportive letters, cards and e-mails coming to us from here and overseas, from colleagues, patients and strangers, from ordinary and famous folk. Most are touching and encouraging, especially those from our patients. One reads:

> 5 years ago I had a termination with you. I am deeply saddened to hear of the violence against you this week.
>
> I just wanted to write and say thank you for your care of me, you were very loving and caring. It has made all the difference in my life.
>
> I found the protestors outside the gate very distressing. Although I am sure that you find them even more of a distress, especially this week.
>
> Please continue your important work.

> Another reads:
>
> I was deeply sorry to hear about one of your security guards getting killed by some pathetic excuse for a man.

It was almost three years ago now that I walked into your clinic and you helped me by terminating a mistake that I unintentionally, but stupidly did to myself. An embarrassed university student from a loving catholic family I was put at ease by the lovely security guards, medical staff and all other employees in your clinic.

As insensitive as this must sound to those protesters that have nothing better to do than sit out the front of your clinic, and to all the other anti-abortionists that exist, not one day goes past that I regret anything I did that day...

I honestly just thank you all continually and pray that you can safely help more and more women through one of life's many challenges.

Another:

After the tragedy that befell you, please keep believing in yourselves with all your hearts. You have helped myself and my husband twice and countless others with your compassion and time. Keep smiling in your eyes and hearts. Thank you for everything you have done...

While June responds to every email, Kate sends out our brief but sincere thanks to those who have sent letters and cards.

Thank you for thinking of us during this difficult time. Our staff have been able to read your words and have felt bolstered and comforted by them.

I also want staff to see all of the correspondence we are sending out, and anything else which will keep them feeling updated, informed and appreciated. June, Joan and Kate help out. Five folders grow bulky and are placed around the clinic for staff to peruse.

A variety of people are propelled by the tragedy at our clinic to phone us or call in personally to express their dismay and offer encouragement to us. Amidst the hundred and one additional tasks now needing to be performed by staff, such contact is welcomed and highly valued. We are aware that people have gone out of their way to make this contact and express their support. It helps renew our faith in humanity.

Four days after the shooting I am down at Libby and David's café to grab a coffee.

'How are you all going down there?' Dave asks. 'Terrible thing.' He is manoeuvring the coffee machine. Stirring the frothy milk in the metal jug. Pouring it carefully into the takeaway cup. Tap tap of the chocolate shaker over it. Plastic cover lid on top, hands it to me.

'Just wait a minute,' he says. 'Got something for you.'

He goes and comes back with a freshly baked Hummingbird cake in large box.

'Tell them all it's from Libby and me. A terrible thing. This'll keep you going.'

It is unexpected. Lovely. Thoughtful. Warm fuzzies. The tears are unexpected too. They are upon me before I realise. The wonderfully generous, caring nature of people.

'Thanks. Thanks David.'

Another morning David tells about the media crew after a newsworthy comment. Did he have a comment about the protesters? 'No,' he'd said. 'Not one you could air.'

Thanks David. Thanks Libby.

The Moving Finger may have written itself into our lives with reckless violence, and we might know nothing about the man responsible, but others are writing themselves into our lives with kindness and courage.

13

Time past and time future
What might have been and what has been
Point to one end, which is always present.
T. S. ELIOT

Terror rips through her veins. He's come back. He's here, in reception. Run, run. June, June. She races to the waiting room. 'He's him, he's him.' Her heart pounds, her whole body shakes. Into June's warm embrace—her gentle words and presence. 'It's okay, Tam. It's not him. They have him in jail. We're here. It's okay, Tammy.' Brings Tam back from the nether world where everyday perceptions distort into malevolent forms with evil intent, back to the comforting reassurance from Lou, too, 'It's okay, Tam, that's a normal reaction.'

Sadly, it is a normal reaction. Normal, but for Tam, highly disturbing and disruptive. It is the memory's recycling of Monday morning's violence, the memory Tam holds in her body, her thoughts, her emotions, her soul. Each has stored its own unique catalogue of experience. At times in synchrony with each other, but like a minor key dirge, at times in the obscure and clashing syncopation created by a disturbed composer, the harsh weirdness of misfired and wildly wired misunderstandings and truths.

The nightmare recedes, images abate, her body shock calms—normality returns. Tam finds herself amongst friends and feels relieved and embarrassed. We marvel at her courage. On Monday, just hours after the shooting, Tam returned to the Clinic to be with us all. Now, less than seventy-two hours after a man was shot in the chest right beside her and Tam faced her own mortality in the most shocking and vile way, Tam is back at her post at reception, doing her job.

Obviously, reception means returning to the scene of the trauma. This is challenging enough in itself, but reception shares with switch a seemingly endless array of triggers for jumpy hyper alertness and fear. People enter and exit, each person expected but surprising, each one a potential threat, the men especially. And sometimes, the ghastly image in her mind is too close to the image meeting her eye. Panic she cannot control.

But Tam stays.

We all hope that Tam will reap the benefits of facing her fears. I pray that the laws of behavioural extinction apply. Tam's confrontation of her fears is closer to the cruelties of flooding than the gentler approach of systematic desensitisation. But to Tam, she is reclaiming her control and power, taking back her life. As surely as she refused to stand passively by and have her life extinguished, Tam refuses to allow the gunman to take over her life now. It is her day to be at work. and she is.

We all keep a close and friendly eye on Tammy, spending more time at reception than we otherwise would. I make reception a makeshift office for the morning, always coming back there between other bits and pieces.

Since the shooting, we have all been thinking of Tam and worrying about her. I was frustrated in contacting Tam because her mobile phone was in her bag and that had to remain at the crime scene. As soon as possible, Janice arranges for a taxi to take it to Tam's home. Tuesday night, Tam phones me, with polite apologies for bothering me. Bothering me? I am relieved and tell her so. We talk for some time. The shooting. Her reactions, then and now. Tam wants to come back to work on Thursday. Her affection for us, and we for her, override her fear, so we devise a plan for her to come in to work, including a lift in with a friend who will walk with her into the Clinic. It will be hard, see how she goes. And she is here. We admire her bravery.

Four days later, a week after the shooting, and Tam already notices an easing of her distress. Images less vivid and less frequent, the basics of eating, sleeping and venturing out are all improving. But it is still hard going, there is an empty, desolate blackness within her. She discovered it one week ago when she was alone, perhaps dead. The threatening blackness engulfs her again at unexpected times.

But Tam fights back against the blackness. Coaxes the sun to shine in its place, plants flowers and shrubs, invites in friendly guests. Tam takes back her life.

Two weeks later, and Tam's family are extremely worried about her working here. Understandably they fear for their precious and beloved daughter's safety. They want her as safe as she can be, please do not go in there, Tam. Tam is torn—she wants to be loyal to us and loyal to her family. But we and Tam know, family must come first. Sadly, but perhaps also with some relief, Tam leaves her job at the clinic.

Some weeks later June organises a farewell afternoon tea for Tam at June's home. We all contribute to the feast. There are home baked cakes, savouries and fruit, champagne, wine, tasty teas and strong coffee. It's fun. We all contribute to Tam's present. With her impeccable taste, June selects a delicate black pearl bracelet, perfect for Tammy. June is still mothering us all, still soldiering on. We don't know how she does it, but we are grateful, although we worry about her.

My conversations with Tam tell me that she has reaped the benefits of her brave return to work, her determination to go for a walk in the park or to play sport, despite her fear. Tam draws on her capacity to trust and confide, her courage, and her loving family and friends who help see her through. She is sleeping and functioning near normal, has a new job which interests her, and is socialising. She is still our sweet Tam, so giving and concerned for others, asking what she can do for us, rather than what we might do for her. I wish for Tam to continue flourishing. I wish for her life to be full of the most beautiful flora, and that she never visits that dark place again.

But there is no avoiding the realities of her life now—the impending court case hangs over her head. Will she have to be a witness? Will she have to see him? When will she know? Who will tell her? When? How? It all refuses to go away. He refuses to go away. I worry for Tam and I worry for others.

But he does not worry. He doesn't worry about anyone, except himself. He continues to maintain his silence for all but necessary day to day inquiries or answers. He refuses to say anything about his crime, anything about who he is. He won't tell police his name or address, age or occupation. He writes long letters, in a neat hand and with intellectual coherence. He is still in control. He is in prison, but he is still calling the shots. Precious police resources being expended just to find out who this Mr X is.

The final identification will be achieved via DNA analysis. People from the small country towns of Orange and Molong in New South Wales will see his photo in the media and provide information leading police to the gunman's home. Samples taken from the gunman will be matched with those taken from his abode. There will be hurried phone calls from Det Snr Sgnt Rovis on the night of Thursday 27 September, to forewarn us and others of the news of his identity which will be published in the morning newspapers—forewarned is forearmed. But not everybody greets the detective with thanks. From one or two, he unfairly suffers angry outbursts at what has happened and how their lives have been irrevocably changed. The detective takes it all in his stride, aware of the unique frustrations and stresses which have been inflicted by the gunman's macabre and cruel game playing. As if this perpetrator's crime has not been enough, the gunman extracts more grief from his victims.

Finally, the shooter's name is published on Friday 28 September 2000, more than two months after Steve Rogers was murdered. Finally, the name which was shared with us some time earlier during an all staff briefing session, reasonably confident it is him. And with it, the gunman's address. The address which also was shared with us in that session, reasonably confident it is his. Finally, after ten weeks of game playing, manipulative, selfish silence, the murderer has a name. It's an ordinary name and a bizarre address. Peter James Knight, aged 47, care of a humpy in the secluded Gumble State Forest, in New South Wales. Take a rugged four-wheel drive 15 kilometres west of Molong, 70 kilometres north-west of Orange, and you might find it. But you wouldn't want to stay.

You'd see the corrugated iron and rough-hewn timber humpy that Knight called home, the fifteen fruit trees and grapevines he tended, the thriving vegetable garden with the metre-high dam he dug using a single shovel. You'd hear from the locals how they remembered him well and called him 'the Yowie'. He never caused any trouble, just went about his business. No idea he held the ideas he did.

In prison Knight is well behaved and speaks when needed. But he continues his silence about himself, his crime and his motives. He is passively uncooperative. He gets rid of his bushy beard and becomes clean-shaven. In prison, he receives no sympathy, and there are reports he is assaulted by other prisoners. Some think he is a good suicide risk. On the evening of Tuesday 2 October 2001, Peter Knight is removed to the Port Phillip Prison Psychiatric unit.

He neither knows nor cares about the sweet Tam's of the world. Nor the grief-stricken mother, the wife so lost, the fatherless children. He doesn't care about the tearful children farewelling their parents to work, 'Don't go to that place.' Does he think of them? The innocent he has harmed? The world he created in his own image? His upside down world of right and wrong where love and goodness are turned on their heads, a world where he believes he has moral outrage on his side, his right to commit an atrocity.

The gunman's heartless, arrogant game playing will continue throughout the Victorian Supreme Court process and proceedings. He will drag it out for as long as he can, informing the court at his committal hearing on 20 November 2001, that he has sacked his lawyer from Legal Aid and will be representing himself at trial. Depending on the judge, this may mean endless delays, drawing out the agony for all those who want and need closure. His tactics rub salt into already stinging wounds.

For us, it seems that someone must know something. To us, so much does not make sense. We keep coming back to anti-choice fanaticism. But why would he come from NSW all the way to our clinic? Why not a clinic in NSW? Why does a man who has lived as a hermit for twelve years, finally embark on such destruction? How does a man with no criminal record end up carrying out the worst crime of all? Why, when he was prone to other obsessions—railing against taking oaths, paying taxes, smokers and tobacco companies—did this one flare into such outrageous violence? What fanned his determination to overcome distance, weapons, discomfort with others, the religious and societal prohibition of murder, to kill Steve and attempt a mass killing?

The homicide detective is back there again. This makes three times, or is it four, to speak to this woman at her Brunswick office? He'll have to check his notes. This sure has been a weird case. Usually you're left with a victim and the chase is on for the murderer, narrowing down suspects, building a case which places the perp at the scene with intent, motive and weapon. This time, they have him in custody from the start, but still there is the chase, the puzzle to find out who he is, establish motive, check whether he has associates, is a patsy used by others, or worked on his own. How often does this happen? The murderer is nabbed at the scene and you end up having more legwork than if he wasn't. And this detective's legwork includes going back to speak to this woman yet again.

Now, finally he leaves with something. After three visits, or is it four? She finally remembers.

Oh, yes he did come to visit her. Yes, the gunman did come to see her. Around Christmas time. Didn't remember at first.

Or on the second visit to question her, or on the third visit, or… thinks the detective ruefully. People. But now…

Oh yes, he did come to visit me. But I sent him away. I didn't like the look of him. Quite odd. Became a bit agitated. Wanted me to read his manifesto or something. Of course I sent him away. I just hadn't remembered until now. Says the woman from Right to Life.

> 'Chairwoman of anti-abortion group Right to Life, said that the man was not attached to her organisation, but such an attack should have been expected.'
>
> *The Age*, 17 July 2001

The day has come. He packs his supplies—his special bag concealing the rifle, another bag with the gags, torches, ammunition, six containers of kerosene, three cigarette lighters, metal devices to jam doors shut, a change of clothes and a handwritten note—about a fatality causing appointments to be cancelled—to stick to the butcher house door and warn off the inevitable sticky beaks. He's all set. Ha!

He cycles to East Melbourne. Mind clear, focused and determined—deadly determined. And He saw everything that He had made and behold it was very good.

He leaves his bike in the rubbish alcove of apartments just one block from the clinic. Rechecks his supplies. Loads seven live rounds into his .30/30 Winchester rifle. Hides it again in his special bag. Checks the gloves already on his hands—trusty old friends. Walks to the clinic. Enters.

In the beginning.

14

We die with the dying:
See, they depart, and we go with them.
T.S. ELIOT

Like the other mornings since the shooting, on Friday 20 July 2001, I am up early and I write. It is quiet and peaceful at that hour. Cosy darkness outside, warmth of the heater inside, a cup of good coffee and the computer screen. A walk afterwards, then refreshed of sorts, ready to face some quick household tasks and get into the clinic.

In at work, I continue what has become my usual routine since Steve's death. I try to get around to every staff member to ask questions, listen, inform, and facilitate healing. Each day there are old topics and new ones. Today, the previous day's debriefing is an obvious topic. How'd you go at yesterday's debrief? Did you find it helpful? What in particular? What not? Did your family find the handouts helpful? How are you sleeping now? Are you still feeling a bit nauseous?

So, for me, this morning fits a similar pattern to the previous days of this week. Except for one big factor which sets my stomach jumping, makes me dress in my best black clothes, and makes me wish I were a million miles away.

Today is the day of Steve's funeral.

So, it is Friday 20th July, the morning of Steve's funeral. It seems fitting that our letter to *The Age* is printed today alongside Steve's photo. In the coming days and months, compliments about the letter come from the most unexpected quarters. I hope it is some comfort to Steve's family, our staff and others.

June's daughter has kindly offered to drive us to Steve's funeral service in Melton. Melton was, I think, conceived as a satellite city and sits less than an hour north of Melbourne. The days since the shooting have taken their toll on all of us, and none of us feel sure about driving safely to the service and back. June, Lou, Susan and I wear black. June is looking forward to the funeral as an opportunity for healing, and for speaking personally with Steve's mother and with his partner. I am dreading it. I find nothing healing in funerals, just pent-up emotion with no outlet. But I too hope to speak with Steve's mother and partner. Like all of us, I see the funeral as an opportunity to pay our respects to Steve and his family.

Finally, just before 10:00am, we gather at switch, my plain funeral finery in stark contrast to the nervous energy within. June's daughter has brought the car around to the front of the clinic and we walk out to the street. And he is there. His face in our faces, his words in our ears. 'How many babies have you murdered today?' And on and on. I cannot believe it. Doesn't he know what day it is? Doesn't he know where we are going dressed in black?

A person watching this scene would think that we do not even notice him. We walk to the waiting car without a word in his direction, not even a glance, so skilled have we become. It does not touch us, we are not moved.

We each slip into the car in turn, and I am flabbergasted. He leans down now, ranting, raving head at the window, hurling words at us, taunting face bobbing at the glass. We, settle into our seats and buckle our seatbelts. But June is cursing under her breath now in dismissive, exasperated whispers. It is only as the car pulls out from the curb that we are free of his abuse.

But this is all quite legal. This is the type of behaviour our political and legal system condones. This is tolerance gone mad. Forget our rights to freedom from harassment. Forget that we are all, in varying degrees, still in a post trauma state. Forget that the women who usually have to face the brunt of their intrusive name-calling often are experiencing high levels of stress all ready, and more so after such attacks. Forget that our political and legal system protects people from harassment within the walls of a business but does not protect its citizens from this chronic harassment. Forget that we are doing nothing illegal and indeed are providing an essential health service, which if not available would see the reproductive mortality rate climb back to devastating levels.

The clinic directors have spent thousands of dollars on legal advice trying to address this shameful situation. We support, with Senator Stott Despoja, the American and Canadian style bubble legislation which prohibits protesters from entering a buffer zone around abortion providing health clinics. It is sensible and practical. But it will require a shift in political, legislative and/or police attitude and practice. It will require society to take its blinkers off and address the issue of abortion as the crucial and personal health issue it is, and address non-criminal instances of violence against women—harassment, stalking, intimidation.

But on Friday 20th July 2001, no such change has occurred or looks likely to occur. It is just another day, where even as we mourn for our work mate shot down in cold blood, we are heckled, insulted and our personal space violated. Just another day when one of the tiny but highly visible and vocal anti-choice groups continues its Godly work.

I am shivering as we approach the chapel which stands opposite a strip of shops with angle parking on both sides of the road. It is already clear that the chapel is bursting at the seams, and people are still arriving. From where we stand at the back of the congregation, near a TV camera, I can see across the sea of bobbing heads to the front pews where Steve's family and close friends sit. I can see Steve's hat from his security guard uniform sitting on top of the coffin. Although he hardly wore it, it leaves a poignant and powerful impression in its personal simplicity.

Long stemmed lilies extend upwards from vases I can't see. The minister enjoins us to be with God. I stand with my arms half folded tightly across my stomach and brace myself for the long haul of words and music and prayer which people have thoughtfully and lovingly arranged and which make not a jot of difference to the senseless waste of it all. To me. Not so for June who embraces this archetypal expression and binding of grief and welcomes its healing aftermath. Not so for Susan who can weep openly and spontaneously and feel some relief. And not so for so many others here today, here to celebrate and give thanks for Steve's life. But not his death.

There are soothing words from the minister and biblical stories and Anglican incantations. Quotes from June's eulogy are included, but her words about feeling angry and Steve being an atheist are diplomatically left out. Laughter and tears accompany stories about Steve told by his close friends, especially the one about Steve and his mate running away to the circus when they were kids. The music with personal meaning flows over us from the small stereo at the front. We glimpse the emotional struggles of those in the front pews. We at the back snuffle and shuffle, cling to our own nearest and dearest. The final slow exit of the coffin, the staggering physical weight on the shoulders of pall-bearers whose spirits are heavy with grief. Hands reach out to touch the coffin's glossy, solid surface. A touch and goodbye. It must be true. The long wait for the funeral procession. More snuffling and hankies. Downcast eyes and sombre faces mingled with the uncomfortable oddity of occasional fleeting smiles of polite recognition between acquaintances. The final disgorging of mourners. spilling out onto the chapel driveway. The hearse loaded with the coffin draped with flowers as if their beauty can camouflage all this bleak sadness and emptiness.

Time goes on. We stand and wait. I am dry eyed but brimming. I cannot wait to leave, it has all taken so long, it just seems to keep going. I realise ashamedly that there is no way I can approach Steve's mother or his partner. June, who is replenished with the communal expression of grief, who is comfortable in this setting, confidently pays our respects to them, and paves the way for future contact. I walk away from the throng and pace up and down the street. Tears blur my vision and my understanding. I finally see the hearse roll slowly out of the chapel driveway and begin its journey to the cemetery. destination known but unknowable.

Back in the car and we are off to the cemetery, but I have already decided I will stay in the car. For me there is no point, it is like punishment, and I am unimportant to it all anyway. I sit in the car and watch from a distance as the others huddle together beneath a sky which now joins in the grief, weeping cold raindrops from heaven. I wish for it to be over.

I do not know it then, but Tim and Rebecca, and Lillian and Sandro are there all together. Ingrid and a colleague are there too.

At last it is over. We are all bundled into the car again, head back to Melbourne. It was a lovely funeral, we say, and speak of this part and that music and that story and this person's contribution and Steve's hat sitting on the coffin and how the minister spoke and how he skipped June's bit about feeling angry and Steve being an atheist, and how hopefully it was all as Steve's mother and partner and children and friends had wanted it to be.

But none of this is what they wanted. We wish it had never happened. Let the moving finger whirl the cold wind of time into disarray, change it so none of it ever happens.

15

We are born with the dead:
See, they return, and bring us with them.
T.S. ELIOT

It is just after 1pm, four weeks and one day post trauma. In my office upstairs, I am sorting through a few last-minute bits and pieces before going home. The phone rings and it is Janice at switch, 'I have Tim on the phone—you know—Tim. He says he is in town for the day and wondered if he could call in. I think you better speak to him.'

Tim Anderson is regarded by clinic staff as a hero, a man to whom we owe everything. None of us really knows him. He is one of the men who subdued the gunman. Janice saw Tim, with Sandro de Maria, holding the gunman down on the floor, and she frantically encouraged them to hold on while they waited interminably for the police and Janice attended to others. Tracey helped clean up and calm down Tim afterwards with a joke and a smoke. Marion considered different styles of paper, artistic designs, wording and organised all of us and our families, so that soon he will receive from all of us a beautiful certificate of thanks with attached words of thanks from everyone's families. Susan, and so many of us, have wanted to give Tim a big hug and thank you. And I have feared for Tim, knowing the enormous impact, disruption and challenges such decisive life-saving action can pose immediately and further down the track.

I feel excited to meet Tim, but aware how difficult this may be for him. We have a brief chat on the phone. He has apparently driven past the clinic a couple of times and has decided he can handle coming inside. He is with his fiancé, Rebecca, and they are just five minutes away. I find out from which direction they will be walking and, hoping to ease the burden somewhat, say I'll walk out to greet them. As I bound past switch, Janice, Susan and Kate are there. 'I'm going to meet them,' I blurt. 'I feel like royalty is coming.'

I walk out on to Wellington Parade, and spot them less than thirty metres away. Although I have not met them before there is no doubt it is them walking hand in hand. Tim is a bearded, reasonably burly bloke in a cuddly bear way. Rebecca, beautifully groomed, seems slight beside him. Our eyes meet and I want to give Tim a hug, but shake his hand, beaming, and then turn to Rebecca and awkwardly hug her. I tell them how pleased I am they have come, but, already into psychologist mode, start commenting on their courage in coming in, the difficulty of doing so, and that we can take as long as we like, and go only as far as feels comfortable. It is Tim's level of discomfort and strength which has been the primary drive behind their visit here today, and it is Tim who will need close monitoring and will determine how far we go today.

I deliberately stop outside the clinic's 118 front gate. We chat on the footpath there for some ten minutes or so. Tim smokes a cigarette and sometimes has to move a little to allow clients through the gate to enter the clinic. I am grateful the anti-choice picketers don't last much past 10.00am every day. Their comments and actions do enough damage to the women and their families trying to access our clinic during their protest times. But in this case, their presence no doubt would have prevented Tim and Rebecca even being able to attempt this hopefully therapeutic, real-life (in vivo) meeting with the place which held so much terror for them just four weeks and one day ago. Then again, I have the distinct impression that Tim would just knock their blocks off.

On a scale of one to 10 for anxiety, Rebecca is around seven, not pleasant by any means but at least manageable. Tim says he is about nine. As we chat and Tim smokes gingerly on a cigarette, Tim's sense of humour and determination shine through and his anxiety level eases enough for him to feel ready to go through the gate and into the clinic's front garden. Half-way up the path I ensure we stop again. Tim and Rebecca both observe how pretty and peaceful the garden is. One of our security guards stands nearby on the garden path leading to 116. Tim sees him and briefly leaves us to speak with him for a few minutes. I am quickly learning more about Tim's determination to stare down his fears.

After another ten minutes and another cigarette, I raise the topic of entering the clinic reception. I reassure Tim that what he has already done has shown great courage, and that it is entirely up to Tim whether he goes any further. I share with Tim and Rebecca my recent conversation with a psychologist being consulted by another survivor in this tragedy. I tell them about my offers to assist in any way—if the psychologist feels that his client has reached the point where returning to the scene would be therapeutic, we could do this in as controlled a way as possible, for example, after hours when no one is around, or during our busiest time, or whatever would minimise even slightly their anxiety. I am highlighting how timing, planning and preparation is the norm, and that people can feel tentative, fearful, need assistance and so on. 'But you,' I tease, 'you just come right on in.' We both know that it is wonderful and gutsy and likely to have positive consequences. We laugh a little and Tim is clear that he wishes to go into the clinic.

Although Tim bravely wears his heart on his sleeve today, he may appreciate a degree of privacy. I go in first to check on the number of clients inside. There are a couple of patients in the waiting room and so I close the door between the reception area and the waiting room. I tell Tim what I have done and give him a mental map of the place, including a safe haven away from the site of the trauma—my room situated through reception and up the stairs. I ready Tim for the likelihood the actual scene and his memory might not tally, his perception of the reception area today might be quite different to the distorted, traumatic memory perceived and stored while his body and psyche were in a state of extreme stress. For example, others who have returned have commented on how bright and light reception seems now compared with then.

I step aside to allow Tim to be the one to open the door into reception. I do not want him to feel that I am hurrying him at all. His pace, his needs, take precedence. The more control Tim has over his return to the site of trauma, the more likely this will be a positive experience for him. Tim opens, enters and stands looking around the reception area. He says it is much lighter than he remembered it, but also observes that it is bigger, particularly the area behind the reception desk. Tim talks through the events as he remembers them. He is sure he heard the sound of breaking glass during the struggle with the gunman, thought the gunman had been pushed through the glass door. In fact, there was no broken glass. There was little in the way of damage to the physical surrounds at all that day. We wonder whether the high-pitched clattering of the venetian blinds against the door while the three men fought might have left the impression of glass breaking.

Tim points towards the filing cabinets where Steve's body fell. I am impressed by Tim's determination to allow himself the time and space to process his experience and to feel and express his emotion. I am also impressed by Rebecca's patient, quiet support. Both Rebecca and I respect the space and silence Tim now inhabits. Tim sits in the chair closest to the closed waiting room door, head bowed. It was just one seat away, the seat just inside the waiting room, where Tim had sat at 10.15am on July 16, not a hint of what was to befall him.

A few minutes later, comfortably seated in the sanctuary of my upstairs consulting room, Tim tells his story, minutely detailed, slow-motion replays, agonising ruminations and recriminations.

Tim tells of being tucked behind the waiting room door, unaware. The rude intrusion of the scuffling Sandro and gunman. Tim's annoyance quickly escalating to decisive action. His quick bond with Sandro. The gun being pointed at him. The physical and psychological replaying of each and every punch. The disbelief and agonising frustration at the gunman's apparent invincibility to Tim's strongest punches. The super-human effort required to finally overpower the gunman. I provide Tim with information about the gunman—his tough subsistence lifestyle, hard manual labour, walking, cycling. Cet Snr Sgnt Rovis' up close and personal assessment that the gunman was extremely fit, robust and almost six feet tall. This guy might have looked dishevelled, he might have been at least fifteen years older than Tim, but he was a man in his physical prime.

Tim listens attentively, meditates on this new information, then continues his detailed, slow-motion replay. He seems exhausted just talking about holding the gunman down on the floor, so mentally and physically draining, it lasted an eternity. The jolting awareness of Steve slumped near the filing cabinets, other people coming into the scene—the guy who runs the gun away from the area, the female doctor trying to revive Steve, the woman shouting orders, the male doctor trying to help Steve and then trying to help Tim and Sandro by sitting on the gunman. The reassurance in such actions and presence. In the retelling Tim jokes that there's never a policeman when you need one—if he'd been up to no good in the city there'd be a squadron in a split second.

But there is also the weight of Tim's guilt and hopelessness at being unable to help Steve, to save his life. I hand him the sheet of clinic letterhead with the quote from Det Snr Sgnt Rovis, which I have already given to other staff struggling with helplessness, guilt, harsh ruminations of doubt:

> 'The fire power he had, even if Steve was
> shot in the arm he would have died from shock.
> That type of weapon has such high velocity—
> shatters bones. He had no chance whatsoever
> being shot in the chest.'
>
> Detective Senior Sergeant Lucio Rovis
> 31 July 2001

Tim reads the quote, studies it for a while and hands it back. He is already unfairly convincing himself that he should have been more aware of what was going on. With his background in pub security he should have been more aware, right at the beginning. He should have been able to read the body language and do something before Steve was killed. Anything to change the course of events. Something he could have done to change things so Steve did not die. Only Tim could possibly see himself and his actions in this light, as having fallen short. Tim was not even in the same room when Knight shot and killed Steve Rogers.

Tim tells of the relief when the police arrive, a woman helping him clean his clothes and taking him outside for a smoke, his silent handshake with Sandro after they have given their police statements. Tim, in his understated way, is at pains to brush off the hero status he has acquired. He is too weary, it is too perplexing. 'I'm just an ordinary bloke.' I suggest that he might have to cop to a compromise from staff, that is, he can view himself as an ordinary bloke, but we will probably always view him as a very, very special ordinary bloke. His smile suggests it's a possibility.

Tim is pleased with my suggestion to look through the clinic further. Rebecca, who has sat quietly and kindly throughout, is happy with this too. We leave my room and cross through the passage to the upstairs staff lounge. Tim cheekily confesses that he had a smoke in there on the day. He talks again about Tracey and how wonderful she was. Down the grand staircase and we are in 116. Admissions, Tim recalls, is where he gave his statement to police and met with Rebecca. When Rebecca was invited to see Tim at the time, she feared that he was hurt or killed. Rebecca now comments on the staff's quick, calm, professional response.

As we walk the complex, I introduce Tim and Rebecca to our staff. At switch, Janice is instantly recognised by Tim as the woman to-ing and fro-ing at the scene, quickly replacing chaos with order. They exchange a warm smile and awkward handshake, like I did almost two hours earlier. I decide that this awkwardness must be what eventuates when you really want to give a big bear hug to someone you don't really know, but a someone who just happened to save your life or the lives of your friends. Susan has no such qualms. She jumps up from behind the switch reception desk and embraces Tim, tears in her eyes. 'I've been waiting so long to do this. Thank you.'

Lou appears. His warm smile, firm hand-shake and thank you is dignified and understated. Its simplicity amplifies the feelings of respect and gratitude. Greg rounds the corner, and Tim recognises him immediately as the first male doctor on the scene. Little chit-chat of shared understandings fills the space of aloneness. There is a bond that is new, yet like slipping into a piece of well-worn clothing. Other staff arrive. One beams from ear to ear, 'I know you.' A warm hand-shake and a reminiscing of sorts ensues. As we walk and stop, greet and chat, the nervous edge is smoothed with humour, warmth and a genuine desire to meet and thank and heal.

Before he leaves, Tim kneels and touches the spot where Steve died.

In the Australian Bravery decorations, announced on 11 August 2002, Tim Anderson was awarded a bravery medal.

That evening at home, I return Lillian Kitanov's phone call from earlier in the day. I have not met Lillian face-to face but have had lengthy phone calls with her. She has the slight nuance in her Australian accent which you associate with an Aussie who has grown up in a household with parents of European extraction. She is obviously intelligent and earnest. Despite the fact her pivotal presence during the shooting at our clinic, our conversations to date have focused on her pregnancy. She has a great deal on her plate at the moment, in addition to the trauma associated with the shooting. I worry about her, given her vulnerability. Yet I sense an affection and solidarity both in her relationship with her partner, Sandro DeMaria and with her family, and Lillian has a fortitude of character that I am hopeful will see her through.

Unprompted, and somewhat unexpectedly, Lillian tells her story of the shooting. Her business-like retelling of the event contrasts with Tim's emotional style. But hers is also typical of a traumatised discourse. Lillian tells her story in a weary stereotypical and unemotional way. Hers is also highly detailed, she switches back and forth from past to present tense and appears driven to get to the end of her story.

There is little doubt that Lillian has ruminated intensely about the 'what if's' and 'should haves', the appalling guilt and responsibility for it all. Lillian changed the appointment time from Saturday to the Monday. They arrived early for the appointment. Lillian was helpless to prevent it. 'I feel more guilty over the security guard's death than Sandro, because before Sandro came in there was just me, the receptionist and the shooter.'

And here it is again. Ordinary, good people taking the blame for what was done by a cold-blooded killer. They believe they should have been able to prevent it, somehow feel it is their fault and they should suffer. Meanwhile the gunman and would-be mass murderer sits quiet and guilt free in his own warped self-righteousness.

In her telling, Lillian emphasises the overwhelming and powerful nature of her experience, the rifle pointed at her pregnant stomach, the look in the gunman's eye, 'You're next'. In a clear reference to God and Lillian and Sandro's close escape from death, Lillian says she feels that 'somebody was with us that day'. She also describes her regression into a psychologically dissociated state of mind. This is quite normal in response to an extreme and abnormal situation, but clinically suggests that Lillian may be faced with a more difficult and complex recovery ahead. Her life now is peppered with paranoia and befuddled with fears.

Although the prevailing popular view is still 'talking about it will help', I am all too aware that talking can also exacerbate post-traumatic stress in some people. It is impossible to interrupt Lillian's retelling, but still, when she finishes, I apologise for any exacerbation of distress her retelling might affect. Lillian responds, 'I've said it so many times. I can repeat the story no problem. But being on my own, that's the problem.' She anticipates that her sleeping problems will be worsened tonight.

I have her permission to speak with her psychologist, and hopefully through this liaison and my own clinical skills, Lillian's retelling will provide her with further opportunities to process the event. I continue to be impressed both by Lillian's courage and by the fracturing in her life caused by her continuing nightmare. She is highly vulnerable, but also resilient.

Slowly over the next few months, Lillian's distressing post trauma state begins to yield to pleasant surprises and bouts of optimism. Lillian and Sandro excitedly anticipate the arrival of their new baby.

> In the Australian Bravery decorations, announced on 11 August 2002, Sandro De Maria was awarded the Star of Courage, the highest honour for bravery.

He sits imprisoned, facing trial. But he is still calling the shots. Not telling them anything. Forcing them to do all the hard slog. Stupid Nazis.

He might be imprisoned, but he is sure of his future. He knows his strategy will get him off. And his mind is free as a bird—free to work and think and plan. He loves the challenge, the mind games, the power he has. And he is incapable of remorse or empathy. The only concern he has is for his own wellbeing. He deludes himself that his causes are for the highest good; that his murderous actions reveal his holy heart. He cannot see that his heart is empty. He cannot see that he has no capacity to love or care for anything or anyone.

But he will prevail. He has all the time in the world. Let 'em wait. He's still in control, just like he was in reception that day. Just like he was when he stole the weapon, gathered his armoury, staked out the clinic. Just like he is now, calculating, calm. Right is still on his side. Let 'em wait for him. Stuff 'em all.

He will sack his lawyer and represent himself. He will draw this out for as long as he can. No one knows better than he. Stuff anybody else. They do not know his stamina and his mental toughness. In prison he has causes revolving about himself which keep him fully occupied. He has Right and God on his side, and injustices to fight. He continues to write lengthy letters—the unusual, disturbing alliance of an orderly and beautiful hand with explicit and violent threats. And he posts it to her. He knows he has an ally in her. He knows she shares his rage—the woman from Right to Life.

'Since they will not be able to find a bully boy with enough guts or stupidity to try and stand over innocent defenders, once I am released, then there will not be an abortionist about the place prepared to remain in operation—guaranteed.'

16

Oh, my Beloved, fill the Cup that clears
Today of past Regrets and future
Fears.
THE RUBAIYAT OF OMAR KHAYYAM

The lawned cliff stretches out towards the sea. The expanse of green drifts into a blue-grey haze of sea and a twilight sky still touched by the sun's long, dying fingers. Across the water lies a slim peninsula where the lights of Melbourne begin to sparkle like a jewelled crown in the sun. Heavenly diamonds are slowly appearing too, first one by one, and then in necklace clusters draping a velvet sky.

It is a mild December evening, and the Fertility Control Clinic Christmas Party is in full swing at Marion's beach-front home, the perfect venue for this end of year get-together. It provides the warmth, freedom of movement and personal setting especially needed this year. Marion is still carrying us along with her good humour, hard work and ability to do. She does it all with her usual class, style and energy. The same wonderful attributes she drew on to conjure up the thank you's to our heroes. The same zest and good-natured generosity we have all drawn strength from over this crazy, tragic year.

A large marquee houses a long table for our festive feast, a small dance floor and a spot for our own Santa Claus to sit and 'ho, ho ho' her way through the giving out of Kris Kringle presents. One of our newest staff members takes on this role with gusto. Strains of music from a small CD player mix with the music of the wind and sea. Tall flag poles on the cliff edge display gaily-coloured flags which flutter in the evening breeze. Staff adorns chairs, and wine glasses adorn tables. Strewn across the lawn in casual, comfortable chaos, we mix and mingle at our leisure.

Kate is in good form. Glamourous, vivacious and full of fun. Is there some sweet symbolism in the rose-coloured glasses she is looking through? As the sun disappears, she pushes the glasses atop her blonde hair, her playfulness undampened. June is talkative and happy. It is fitting that June was the 'captain' on the bus which brought many staff from the clinic to Marion's tonight. A bus ride full of laughter and champagne. Susan is elegant and sparkling, her laughter like crystal on the evening air. Lou moves easily amongst us, with cheeky wise cracks and warm hugs.

At times Marion is like a tour guide, taking small groups of us down the steep steps of the cliff to the sea below. Here we breathe in the soft lapping of the waves gently touching the bank before receding again. We watch the flight of a large water bird as it gracefully soars, then descends to skid onto the silver-streaked water. From smooth gliding, to wings all aflutter, to a sedate repose. We are blind to the quick paddling of webbed feet under the surface. All is serene tranquillity here. We embark on the adventure down to the sea with little thought to the exertion required to climb our way back up the cliff's primitive steps. But we make it, with talking and laughing and deep, panting breaths, back to the convivial warmth of partying with friends.

It is Saturday 15 December 2001. Few here tonight think of this date as stretching back to, or away from, the 16 July 2001. For a while our lives were inextricably defined by time before, and time after, 16 July 2001. For some outside the clinic, Steve's death, the shooting, continues to be the dominant fracture dividing then from now. For others it is just one more fracture in the continuity of their lives. One more move on a chessboard of nights and days where destiny plays with their lives. Where the shooting and murder of Steve dims in the wake of subsequent twilights turning into night, and dawns dazzling into new days.

On this night, looking up into the deep sky above, one can see where all time is intertwined. Where past, present and future mingle. And just at that point, where the deepness engulfs all, a brightness emerges and a neat pattern takes shape. The dark dome of the sky transforms to an art deco ceiling where large plaster flowers sit in relief in a white criss-cross pattern and descending from the central square is a chandelier of some thirty or more round white globes interlinked by brass. Beneath is a setting reminiscent of the theatre where storytellers' fictional dramas are played out by costumed actors. But the dramas played out in this theatre are not fiction. They are real. Amidst dignity and ritual, polished wood and maroon fabrics, this is where ugly and evil secrets are revealed to the public. This is Victoria's Supreme Court, Banco Court, Court One. Nine months after the events of 16 July 2001, on 15 April 2002, Peter James Knight is standing trial for murdering Steve Rogers.

The audience climbs the back stairway to the public gallery to look out over the courtroom stage from up in 'the gods'. The protagonists enter below, step onto the rich carpet and sit on the cushioned seats. The legal eagles are donned in wigs and gowns.

Tailored in red with grey trim, the judge sits centre stage on his grand throne, blue velvet curtains pulled back on either side. With their back to the gallery, barristers and assistants clutter the tables facing the judge. The defendant sits hidden in the dock beneath the audience and with full view of the rest of the court. Jurors file in right stage, the media squeeze in left, witnesses come and go up the steps to the small witness box. And the drama unfolds.

At times, the sheer weight and length of proceedings suggests that whoever designed this court had themselves spent hours in courtrooms. For there is the hint of the bored mind at work in an architectural theme of noughts and crosses. The ceiling squares are nine, a giant grid for tic-tac-toe. The numerous ornate flowers are nothing but disguised noughts, and along the sides of the three tall windows gracing each wall, are four decorative crosses. All the tools for a simple game of strategy, to beat the dullness, to be played against oneself for amusement, or against an opponent for competition.

The only signs of modernity denting the old-world charm of this court are the two TV screens sitting high on the wall above the media, the overhead projector, lap top computers and microphones. It is quite staggering that, unlike the County, Magistrates and other courts where visitors must pass through metal detectors and security guards, the Supreme Court has no such security. Anyone, it seems, has unfettered access through a rather disappointingly small and plain doorway. Though murders and mayhem are the real-life stories of the day, the possibility that any like actions could be acted out within these reverential walls is apparently not countenanced. For the victims presenting themselves to the Supreme Court, such an absence of security is glaring and mystifying. Although security is tight around the defendant, there is apparently little or no thought to the possibility of others intruding violently into such respectful and orderly proceedings.

Today, and for the next four days, the defendant represents himself and concedes nothing. Each person who gathered evidence, from clinic floor plans to photographs to DNA, must be called to testify to every minutiae of evidence. Each person who witnessed the atrocity of 16 July tells their abbreviated story in response to the Crown Prosecutor's questions. Some keep their gaze focused at the jury, the judge or the prosecutor, some are driven to look at him. There is minimal relief that the defendant staring back at them is so changed physically—no beard, clean, neatly dressed, younger—that they can almost believe they are not confronting the murderer.

The defendant declines to cross-examine any witness or to call any witness. There are four days of uncontested evidence.

On 22 April 2002, Knight begins his address to the jury. His voice explodes into the solemnity of the Melbourne Supreme Court with the same ruthless brutality as the bullet he directed into Steve's chest.

'At last. At Last!'

In thirty hours' time when the jury returns a guilty verdict and is excused, his voice erupts again. Unrepentant and threatening towards the judge.

'You will be made to pay the penalty.'

Between these two shocking outbursts, is a lengthy and detailed address to the jury, consistent only in its unrelenting bullying and grand-standing. He cruelly denigrates and ridicules his victims and those who have worked so tirelessly to bring him to justice. He exudes intimidating, self-righteous indignation as he tells blatant lies. He is so smug and superior, in his intellect, his morals and his wit.

I am sure that no one has ever before hurled such insults at Chief Crown Prosecutor Bill Morgan-Payler, QC, as Knight does now. Knight rants that the prosecutor has presented a case which is 'bloody useless', has 'no brains at all', and 'is a good example of how a barrister should not get a witness to give evidence'. At one point, Knight challenges the prosecutor to 'stand up and call me a liar…' and when the prosecuting team remain absolutely unmoved, Knight derisively says, 'No response—well!'

Knight works through each of the accounts of the Clinic witnesses, denigrating and ridiculing with sarcastic glee, 'What a witness. She is awful! Where shall I begin with this one?'

And it is all so disturbingly clear. On display from beginning to end is this man's pathetic claim to humanity. He is incapable of any degree of empathy. He has no remorse for the appalling crime he has committed, for the shocking impact of his actions. His callous disdain for others, his arrogant sense of omnipotence and pathetic attempts at cleverness set him on the evil course which sees him now in the dock of the Supreme Court. No one can doubt the Chief Prosecutor's assertion that Knight went to the Clinic 'with murder on his mind'.

There is a sad realisation amongst some here that at some point, that at some stage in his life, this murderer was but a child. The events, the unknowable linkages between then and now, between genetic predisposition and society's input, between ugly quirks of nature and tragic environmental glitches. What went so horribly wrong? This pathetic, incredibly dangerous man poses daunting and worrisome questions for our society. How did we as a society fail him? The family and the school, expected to provide protection, love and encouragement to children, can sadly sometimes be the most punitive and damaging to children. Sometimes no matter how loving and stable, the inherent temperament of a child can pose insurmountable problems for the normally 'good enough' family or school. Is the child destined to grow into what has been genetically pre-programmed no matter what society provides?

Similar questions must be asked about the factors impacting on Knight's transformation from socially isolated, but nonetheless harmless, adult, to an adult who has 'murdered one man, in the context of having planned a massacre of many', as Justice Teague will so eloquently describe Knight's ghastly actions during sentencing. Does society's failure to protect women from bullying anti-choice protesters legitimise the protesters' stance and rhetoric to the point where another vulnerable person feels encouraged to put into action a plan consistent with that extreme rhetoric? If society in general validated and respected women's reproductive rights instead, fulfilled its duty of care to women and their families accessing a health clinic, might Knight's crusade never have ended so tragically?

These are daunting but important questions. Just as daunting is the chance that the unremorseful, cold and calculated killer Knight is now might one day be released back into society.

Although we might all label Knight 'crazy' given his shocking crime, and grandiose and antisocial behaviour, the legal definition of crazy is quite different to our everyday notions and has serious sentencing consequences. Justice Teague, so diligently trying to ensure that Knight is not disadvantaged by Knight's determined stance to defend himself, and so diligently trying to ensure no opportunity for an appeal at the end of all this, calls for pre-sentencing psychiatric assessment.

The result is conflicting psychiatric opinion from which markedly differing sentencing consequences ensue. My understanding is somewhat stymied by my academic studies comprising the outdated McNaughton's Law and the plea of insanity, rather than the Crimes Mental Impairment Act introduced in 1997. This legislation runs to eighty-four pages and deals with a host of issues including the defendant's state of mind at the time of the offence, the defendant's fitness to be tried at the time of trial, and the dangers of diagnoses based on cultural aspects such as a person's religious beliefs.

In the one corner is Dr Senadipathy. His report argues that Knight fits the criteria for the diagnosis of Paranoid Schizophrenia. This is a psychotic illness. Knight is mentally ill and as such deserves the protection of the court rather than blame. Although highly dangerous, Knight cannot be held responsible for his actions because he is suffering an illness which controls his behaviour, makes him unable to appreciate the nature of his crime, and the consequences of his action. Because of his mental illness, he cannot differentiate between right and wrong, reality and fantasy. He is ill and our justice system does not blame the ill. It provides care for them. If Dr Senadipathy's opinion is accepted by the court, Knight will be kept at the Governor's pleasure in psychiatric care until such time as Knight is assessed as no longer being a threat to society.

In the other corner is Dr Barry-Walsh. His report argues that Knight is not suffering a psychotic illness. Dr Barry-Walsh describes Knight as having a 'peculiar and paranoid personality'. Although clearly odd and extremely dangerous, Knight is not mentally ill. As such Knight should be judged and sentenced for his crime according to the normal criteria.

Given these conflicting psychiatric reports, on Thursday 26 July 2002, the case is adjourned yet again to allow for the psychiatric evidence to be examined and tested in person in the

Supreme Court of Melbourne. Two weeks later, on Thursday 8 August 2002, two psychiatrists take their turn in the witness box at the Supreme Court. Dr Senadipathy has had the apparent advantage of seeing Knight weekly for some eight months. This compares with Dr Barry-Walsh's two-hour interview with Knight and information gleaned from other sources, including a conversation with Dr Senadipathy and psychiatric unit observation notes. Whose opinion would you back? One might conclude easily, Dr Senadipathy's. Not necessarily so. As one who has assessed families at the Children's Court Clinic over just four- or five hours face-to face, with recourse to other sources of information, I know that two hours is ample time to make an insightful and valid assessment. It is the repeated careful and intensive listening to the person and the wealth of information contained in just one one-hour interview which can result in a meaningful whole appearing, like pieces coming together to form a puzzle.

Dr Senadipathy is cross-examined aggressively by the Chief Prosecutor for over an hour. Dr Senadipathy's assessment that Knight's beliefs are delusional and therefore Knight was unable to exercise choice since delusional beliefs leave no capacity to choose, are challenged vigorously. The prosecuting team argues convincingly that, to the contrary, Knight has 'strongly held beliefs'. These strongly held beliefs are different from the majority but not different in quality from the beliefs of other people who we do not deem delusional—devotees of religious orders, people from the '60s who dropped out to drop in to communes, other abortion activists in the United States who have killed, the fanatical religious suicide bomber... Dr Senadipathy's argument appears to be somewhat circular and a little confusing in that it is in part the nature of Knight's crime which seems to define Knight's thought processes as delusional. In addition, there is an absence of other usual indicators of the very serious illness of schizophrenia. There is no evidence that Knight experiences auditory or visual hallucinations, self-referential ideas (e.g. thinks the TV newsreader is speaking directly to him), or thought disorder, although Dr Senadipathy refers to Knight having 'systematised beliefs' and 'loose knit associations.' Dr Senadipathy agrees with the prosecution's suggestion that Knight may not have been true and frank with him and from time to time may have played games with him. But Dr Senadipathy will not be budged from his diagnosis.

Dr Barry-Walsh spends only twenty minutes on the stand. He is a most accomplished and balanced witness and I am partial to his sentiments and argument. He clearly states that Knight 'does not have a mental illness which requires treatment'. Knight holds strong beliefs, is prepared to act strongly on them and feels it is his right to act in a very violent way. There are no indications of poor impulse control. In fact quite the contrary, given his degree of organisation. There is no evidence of mental decline. Even in childhood Knight was a shy loner. There is no evidence of disordered thinking. Knight does not lack the usual coherence of thought seen in normal people. There are no signs of 'loose' thinking typically seen in schizophrenia where apparently random or idiosyncratic linkages lead to incoherence. Unlike Dr Senadipathy, Dr Barry-Walsh can clearly define a 'delusion' and differentiate it from merely a strongly held belief. A delusion is 'absurd, bizarre, unlikely or untrue' and its origin is also bizarre, for example, the TV newsreader tells him he is Jesus Christ. Dr Barry-Walsh is rightly troubled by Knight's beliefs being labelled delusional because they stem from biblical scripture. In Dr Barry-Walsh's opinion, Knight was 'acting with full understanding of how society viewed his actions and he felt he was morally justified' and Knight 'doesn't fit the criteria' for treatment set out in the Sentencing Act.

I particularly liked Dr Barry-Walsh's response to the question of risk, 'I think the Court does not need much instruction from a psychiatrist [as to that].' But Dr Barry-Walsh pointed out that despite Knight's openness with him, Knight was also 'very closed' around the actual offence. 'One cannot really know what was in his mind around the crime…' Dr Barry-Walsh could, 'not discount that Mr Knight might have harboured delusional beliefs at times, or now, and may experience some mental disorder. But, the weight of evidence is not consistent with him suffering from a psychotic illness, schizophrenia.'

In contrast to the disparate diagnoses, which share a great deal of common ground and whose ambiguity may rest with the flaws in the current psychiatric taxonomy, there is in fact considerable agreement between the two psychiatrists. Both agree that Knight knew that as far as the law is concerned the crime itself was wrong, understood that what he did was wrong by society's standards, understood the charge, was competent to instruct a lawyer, is highly dangerous, and treatment options and outcomes are pessimistic.

Still, Justice Teague is dictated to by the Act. He is still cornered, the 'grey' of the medical opinion troubles him. 'I'd prefer to get a dark grey or a light grey.' Yet another adjournment, another delay, another day out for Knight, another frustration for his victims. We wait yet again for another psychiatric opinion to be proffered, that of Professor Paul Mullen. Knight's importance is again highlighted, that of his victims denied. I see Shirley, Steve Roger's mother, sitting below in the Court room. Still no sign of closure for those suffering most from Knight's murderous behaviour—if closure can ever really occur.

But there are signs that Knight too has finally had enough of the courtroom. He writes to Justice Teague asking that he be sentenced without further delay. There are reports Knight is being sedated.

But on 22 April 2002, in the magnificence of the Melbourne Supreme Court, Court One, as we hear Knight's voice for the first time, and as we watch from a point of view divorced from the Crimes Mental Impairment Act and the psychiatric profession's framework, it is all so clear. As long as you can see past Knight's authoritative and intimidating stance. Push yourself through the obsessive details and contrived connections he passes off as clever logic. And recognise the perverted role he has created for himself of superior teacher and director to his clearly intellectually feeble cast of witnesses, jury and bench, 'I'll explain to you what that means…', his superiority at times inspired by biblical wisdom, 'I bring you good news…'

And through it all, now in his closing address, Knight cleverly manages to make an unsworn statement where he tells his version of events to the jury without the opportunity for that version to be cross-examined. There is to be much talk during pre-sentencing examination of psychiatric opinion that Knight's declining to cross-exam any witness reflects the defendant's beliefs, biblical in origin, about the folly of taking an oath. It is the opinion of Dr Senadipathy that in fact this belief is of a delusional quality and is responsible for Knight's withdrawal from everyday social commerce and for his murderous actions. But rationalising his abnormal and antisocial behaviour through ideas of moral and religious superiority is merely symptomatic of Knight's psychopathy. The real reason Knight does not cross-examine or does not take the stand on his own behalf is simple. Cross-examination does not allow him to retain total control. He cannot be fully prepared for how a witness may respond, or how the prosecutor may respond. And the mystery and tragedy of this man is that he must be in control—totally, completely and arrogantly. His grandiosity, need for admiration and lack of empathy is on display for all to see. He reeks of narcissism, a term coming from the Greek mythological story of Narcissus who fell in love with his own reflection and then pined away.

It is clear that Knight has seen himself as the puppeteer pulling the strings of we, his puppets, making us dance to his tune, over months of his thwarting the investigation via passivity, mysterious silence, and his decision to represent himself. We can only marvel with relief and gratitude that he did not get his chance to play out the complete role of the puppeteer on 16 July 2001.

But initially, on 22 April 2002, it is not clear at all. After months of almost total public silence, the jury, the media, and the rest of the public gallery are jolted by the sudden aggressive authority of Knight's address. They sit like reprimanded students, struggling to take in their professor's cruel dissection of their grossly inept exam answers, the truth lurking somewhere out of reach, cloaked in supercilious rhetoric and sarcasm.

Lillian Kitanov sits beside me in the public gallery. Like most here she is concentrating intently, struggling to take it all in. She is growing more anxious, misunderstood, and retraumatised as she tries to take in his criticism of her testimony. 'The way he shot the security guard, so cool and calm, I was basically just waiting to get shot,' Lillian told the court. He is still treating her as an object to be ruthlessly flung out of his way. He has no understanding of the trauma he has, and is, causing her. He is intent on attacking her again, ridiculing her testimony, revealing supposed inconsistencies.

Laboriously quoting from the case transcript, he twists and corrupts her testimony. He distorts the events of Steve's murder and Lillian's shocking experience of it.

Lillian is clearly upset. I am furious. Hasn't he hurt her enough? I lean over towards Lillian and whisper in her ear, 'He's a bully, Lillian. You have done nothing wrong. You did great. He is on trial. This is all rubbish. He's a dangerous bully who thinks he's superior to all of us.'

After half an hour of Knight's insulting diatribe, I decide I have wasted enough of my time on this dangerous, pathetic man. I wish that everyone else could leave too, deprive him of his audience.

Thirty hours later, on 23 April 2002, Knight is found guilty of murdering Steven Rogers at the Fertility Control Clinic on 16 July 2001. On 17 September 2002, Knight is deemed not to be mentally ill, and on 23 November 2002, Knight is sentenced to life imprisonment with a minimum non-parole period of 23 years.

You will be made to pay the penalty.

The Supreme Court fades back to the inky sky of 15 December 2001. There has been no court case. None has stood as witness in the dock of the Supreme Court to answer the questions of the Chief Crown prosecutor, to face yet again the events of Steve's murder, to tell it all again this time in the presence of the gunman. None have visited the Offices of the Public Prosecutor to have anxieties associated with the grandeur and mystique of our justice system quelled by the gentle competence and reassurance of the prosecuting team—Bill Morgan-Payler, Rosemary Carlin and Kylie Duthie. And none of what we know to be the truth has been tested in a court of law. The gunman sits in a prison psychiatric unit, imprisoned in a mind we do not fathom and because of actions reprehensible. We do not think of him. We remember Steve in our hearts and we think of Steve's family fleetingly. We get on with our lives and help others get on with theirs. It is what we do.

On the first anniversary of Steve's death, 16 July 2002, we hold a special afternoon tea in the gentle surrounds of what we call the 'recovery lounge'. The couple of staff who have left return for the occasion. We gather with glasses of wine and plates of comforting food and catch up with each other's lives. June is dressed in her shimmering jacket with the purple cuffs, her celebrant garb. June draws on her consummate skill as a celebrant, counsellor, communicator and wise human being, to speak of everything as it should be spoken. With sensitivity, warmth, humour and optimism. And June begins:

> *It is twelve months ago now that we were all gathered in this room feeling, or perhaps not feeling, a range of emotions. I think it would be safe to say that numbness and disbelief were among the range of feelings. And I think maybe a closeness and feeling of solidarity among those of us who had worked here together for a long time. I can't imagine what some of the newer members of staff were feeling, probably something like, 'What the hell am I doing here?' But it is great to see that two of the newer members then are still with us today.*
>
> *It has been a difficult year for all of us. After the initial shock came the waiting for identification and then the long*

wait until the trial. When it finally started and the horror of that day was once again before us I think many of us suffered more than we had immediately after the event.

This is a stressful field to work in under normal circumstances but I feel that the added stress of the last twelve months has been evident with the number of people who have succumbed to illness recently. We had hoped that by now Peter Knight would have been sentenced but hopefully that day won't be too far away and we then can close that chapter of our lives and finally put it behind us. We will never forget that awful day but maybe we no longer have to dwell on it. As time goes by and the publicity dies down, less people talk about it and we can file it away in our memory.

I would like to thank Susie for all the support she has given staff from the day of the tragedy to the present time. I feel that without her immediate actions and tireless effort over the past twelve months we would not have come out of it as well as we have. I would also like to thank Lou, Ian and Greg for the support they have given the staff. I know the costs have been quite substantial and it was gratifying to know that no expense was spared to provide counselling and added security in the ensuing months after the incident. I would like to publicly thank Lou's wife for the support she gave us on the day. She came straight into the clinic on hearing of the shooting. Now I know her first thought was probably for her husband but through the day she made numerous cups of tea and her presence and support was appreciated.

I think too that all the staff should be congratulated on the way they conducted themselves on that day. There was no hysteria and I believe the police made comment about the calmness of the staff. The staff has always been there for one another and this mutual support has gone on as usual throughout this last year. We can always find something to laugh about, be it just the bizarre names of the children of some of our clients or Kate's fabulous cartoons. But we can always manage to keep morale high. And this was more important than ever over the past twelve months.

So before we do let go of this let us just take a moment to think about Steve who lost his life on that day and to think about Sandro, Tim and Brett who were the real heroes on the day. We know that without their part in the drama the outcome could have been far worse and we owe our lives to them. So we will now observe a minute's silence in memory of Steve and the sacrifice he made that day.

June's words still float through us as we each turn inward to our own thoughts and memories of Steve, our grief for his family, our thanks for our own lives, our other heroes, individual streams of consciousness flowing from then to now. Then June's voice brings us back to the present, and back to a future of optimism and cherished reality.

And now on a more positive note I would like to remind you that this year, 2002, marks thirty years since the concept of this clinic began in some very ordinary rooms just down the road at 106 Wellington Parade. The original building was demolished some years ago now but let me tell you it was not pretty. But when Bertram Wainer opened those rooms in 1972 it was the first time that women in Victoria could talk openly to a doctor about their problem of an unplanned, unwanted pregnancy without feeling like a criminal. It began a whole new era. Back then the patients were sent, after their initial consultation, either to Dr Levin in St Kilda Road or to Dr Bayliss in Albert Street East Melbourne for the procedure. The three finally formed a partnership and came into the building at 118 Wellington Parade in late 1974. Bert in his wisdom saw fit to employ the very young Louis Rutman back in those early days.

There were difficult times leading up to the establishment of the clinic and there have been some difficult times throughout those years, including a raid by the Federal Police and various ugly demonstrations. The ultimate in difficult times has been the tragedy that occurred last July but it is now time to affirm that we are not going to be cowed by this, as we have not by any of the past events. Those who have worked here over the years have generally been strong people who were willing to stand up for what they believed in. I think our present staff gives credence to this statement and should all be proud of what they have contributed to the cause of freedom for women. The work we do is important, not just for women but often for the preservation of the family unit and for the welfare of existing children. Don't ever underestimate the value of your work and the importance of the survival of this clinic and others like it. I know that Bert Wainer would be proud of you all today, to know that the clinic he started after the long struggle of 1969 and 1970 is still going strong and still upholding the ideals that he set out to achieve at the beginning.

The famous pioneer of birth control in the early part of the 20th century, Margaret Sanger said in 1920, 'No woman can call herself free who does not own and control her own body. No woman can call herself free until she can choose consciously whether she will or will not become a mother.'

Later in the century, about 70 years later, Ruth Ginsberg said, 'A woman's right to choose an abortion is something central to her life, to her dignity and when governments control that decision for her, she's being treated as less than a full adult human being responsible for her own choices.'

Both of these statements seem fairly obvious I'm sure, to all of us here today and should seem that way to any intelligent person. However there is still the minority out there who don't see it this way and want to impose their views. Even in 2002 we still have to maintain the vigil and make sure that these rights and freedoms are not taken away from us. We've come this far, we will continue in the future. Let's raise our glasses and drink to us. We have much to be thankful for today.

Glasses are raised. Thanks are given. And the staff Christmas party, 2001, bubbles along. In the marquee, on the lawn overlooking the sea, one of the clinic Directors speaks poignantly about our difficult year, our rallying together, how well we've done. He clearly has given this considerable thought and I, like others, appreciate his words. We all deserve them, I think.

Janice wears a tailored trouser suit and is relaxed and engrossed in conversations with staff and friends. As usual Janice is interested in where we and our families are all at—Janice, who carries a rather awesome responsibility in ensuring the smooth running of Australia's first and largest free-standing, women-centred, abortion providing clinic where women access medical treatment for a wide range of fertility-related health services. But on this wonderful evening beside the sea, the air so fresh, the company so warm, I see her, in my imagination, dressed in a sixties' two-piece bikini and doing the twist with Elvis on a paradise beach.

He is lashed to a trolley, standing up right, his hands cuffed, and wheeled into Victoria's Court of Appeal. On 25 March 2004, this is how authorities must deal with Knight's refusal to appear at a hearing to consider his application to be granted an extension of time to file a notice of appeal. His application for leave to appeal against conviction (out of time) was refused by the Registrar of the Court of Appeal on 18 November 2003—a decision made by the Registrar in his chambers, not in open court. Knight is now asserting his right to have his application heard by three judges in the Court of Appeal.

Once the proceedings commence, he finds his voice—the judge presiding over his Supreme Court trial had been 'not nearly learned enough' and 'dimwitted', the jury was not impartial and only a jury comprising people opposed to abortion were capable of judging him…

The three Court of Appeal Judges unanimously reject his bid to appeal out of time. It is finally over.

Perhaps he dreams. The eucalyptus vapour hangs heavy and fresh in the dampness of the early morning. He gazes upward into the blue infinity of the sky. Drawn up to meet it. Flying, light as a feather, at one with the angels. He is free of the heavy weight of the bodily world, flying in white holiness into the blue with the air deliciously vitalizing as it swirls past him. He travels deeper towards his ecstatic rebirth where the blue now deepens to indigo and the stars appear.

His life washes past him and through him, cleansing and pure. Yes, he belongs with the angels. Why, he belongs with the Gods. He is perfection. He is Truth. Spreading the Good Word through his Good Deeds.

The jarring body blow of the gumtree as it slams him back to earth. Lying now with its great weight upon him, can't breath, can't move. Numb panic. Betrayed.

All these months imprisoned. The bastards. Knowing all the time how crucial his task and how pivotal his role to the purification of mankind. They think they can trip him up, they think he isn't savvy to their tricks and charms. The bastards.

Oh, he'd had fun with them. Not always let on that he knew. Played along, turned the tables on 'em and they didn't even realize. Stupid idiots. He was up to their games. He just had to become ever more vigilant. He knew they were using high-tech surveillance equipment to watch his every move. The whole thing was a set up. They thought they could get him. The bastards.

He knew his food was threatened—the very substance that sustains him. Of course they'd contaminate that. But they can't make him eat. He isn't like other mere mortals. He has conditioned himself. Don't they realize he can go without the poison that is their world, the poison that is their food. He will be cleansed, and he will sacrifice himself for their sins. He will show the bastards.

Let he who has no sin cast the first stone. The lusting whores. Nazi dogs lapping at the feet of the abortionists. The message is for me and me alone, you idiots. You think you can trick me, you bastards. I won't say a bloody word. I won't eat a morsel. You can't get me. Get out. What bloody thing are you saying? What are you saying? I am doing God's work. See here I've written it down. Shut up you bastards. The pain. And ye shall find paradise in the House of the Lord.

The hands upon him. The drugs pour into his blood stream. The deathless dream.

Postscript

In the Australian Bravery decorations, announced on 11 August 2002, Steve Rogers was commended posthumously, Tim Anderson was awarded a bravery medal, and Sandro De Maria was awarded the Star of Courage, the highest honour for bravery.

On Tuesday 19 November 2002 Peter Knight was sentenced to life imprisonment with a minimum non-parole period of 23 years. On 25 March 2004, any chance of appeal was rejected.

Simon Brown-Greaves' Occupational Health Services and Deb Glowaski moved on to CISM roles in the wake of the September 11 terrorist attacks in America and the collapse of Ansett airlines in Australia.

The clinic was catalysed by Steve's murder to campaign for abortion safe access zones. On Friday 27 November 2016, the Victorian Parliament finally enacted Safe Access Zones legislation.

The High Court of Australia's decision in support of the legislation saw abortion safe access zones roll out across Australia.

The Fertility Control Clinic continues to provide the highest standards of care to the women of Australia and their families.

A commemorative plaque now sits in the clinic garden:

Steven Gordon Rogers
8-10-1956 to 16-7-2001
Always Remembered

Acknowledgements

I am again so grateful to my publisher, Michael Wilkinson, for his encouragement to re-release *Murder on His Mind* with *Empowering Women.*

James Weston and Dan McDonnell were instrumental in the original *Murder on His Mind* manuscript finally reaching the safe and experienced hands of Michael Wilkinson who recognised the story's powerful layers and provided me with the reassurance, know-how and confidence to see the book first brought to the public in 2006. Back then, Wilkinson Publishing's Berith Ostrom was a delight to work with, and editor Carolyn Ford ultimately pushed me towards a better final product.

In 2021, Michael's belief in both books has been inspirational, and associate publisher Jess Lomas has been a treasure and joy to work with on both *Murder on His Mind* and *Empowering Women.* Thanks must also go to Wilkinson Publishing's Sue-Ann Miller, Cassie Chiong, and to Alicia Freile for the book cover designs utilising the work of Kupritz.

With this new edition of *Murder on His Mind*, I again thank all those people who told their story. Hue Luu, Lillian Kitanov and Tim Anderson generously and intimately shared their story, as did clinic staff members who have contributed to the clinic over many years and who were particularly caught up in this tragic event: Lou, Janice, Susan, June, Kate, Marion, Vicki, Hue, Greg, Kathy, Ian, Joan, Tracey, Ingrid, Leanne, Angela, Priya, and Patricia. Fertility Control Clinic staff encouraged me to write this story and I appreciate their support. Special thanks to June Dryburgh for allowing me to draw on her wisdom and reproduce in full her clinic memorial service.

Steve Rogers' selfless actions saved the lives of my friends, colleagues and so many others. For this I, with countless others, are eternally grateful to Steve, but also will forever regret the devastation for Steve's family of his needless death. Warmest thanks to Tony, Darryl and Tariq who were the clinic's main security guards over many years and carried out their duties with sensitivity and good humour.

The police worked tirelessly to ensure staff was kept informed and a just outcome would ensue. The Office of the Public Prosecutions, especially Kylie Duthie, sensitively and diligently kept us apprised of progress in the court case. His Honour, Justice Teague, presided over the court proceedings and provided a concise yet comprehensive account in sentencing, R v Peter James Knight [2002] VSC 498.

Senator Natasha Stott Despoja's continuing interest in the clinic extended to writing the original foreword, included here again, with her usual flare and amidst a heavy workload. I thank her for this. I also thank her for so generously writing the foreword to *Empowering Women*, and for her many years of determinedly fighting the good fight for women, which of course is a fight that benefits everyone.

Dr Patricia Brown painstakingly read an early draft of the book, offered astute and kind comments, and continued to encourage me in this undertaking. Leslie Cannold provided me with the clarity and perspective I needed to persist in my efforts to bring this story to the public. I have been so fortunate to have author mentor, Myf Jones, nourishing me with both wise counsel and cheer leading of my efforts, no matter what other demands she faces. Lizzie O'Shea has provided the optimism, inspiration and insight I craved.

Finally, my heart goes out to my family: without your patience, support and understanding this story would never have been told, and the events described in *Empowering Women* would never have happened.

my clients, no matter what other demands she faced. Lizzie O'Shea has provided the optimism, inspiration and insight I craved.

Finally, my sincere apologies to my family without your patience, support and understanding this story would never have been told, and the events described in [illegible] would never have happened.

About the Author

Susie Allanson B.A. (Hons. Psychology), M. A. (Clinical Psychology), PhD, was a clinical psychologist in Melbourne for almost forty years, and the clinical psychologist at the Fertility Control Clinic for twenty-six years. Susie's clinical work also focused on children and families in settings such as the Royal Children's Hospital, Children's Court Clinic, schools and her private practice. She has served on the Board of Family Planning Victoria and various committees, been a supervisor and reviewer, and has spoken and written about pregnancy and abortion in various forums and in professional journals. Susie is the author of *Empowering Women: From Murder & Misogyny to High Court Victory* with lawyer Lizzie O'Shea, and the novel *Genevieve Knows Too Much*.

Also by the author

Empowering Women

By Dr Susie Allanson with Lizzie O'Shea

Empowering Women is the uplifting behind-the-scenes story of how the murder of a man catalysed one abortion-providing clinic's fight to protect women from religious extremists. An army of women responded and forced Parliament to enact a women-centred law that ultimately saw a 2019 landmark High Court decision enshrine Australian women's entitlement to reproductive autonomy and respect.

Empowering Women gives you a front row seat in the courtroom and takes you behind closed doors into the personal, legal and political twists and turns of this long campaign. Interwoven with Susie's personal narrative are insights from key protagonists, primary source material, and crucial lessons for anyone wanting to change the law or redesign the world for the better.